The Stages of Life

The Stages of Life

~~~

A Groundbreaking Discovery: The Steps to
Psychological Maturity

Clifford Anderson, M.D.

THE ATLANTIC MONTHLY PRESS
NEW YORK

Published simultaneously in Canada
Printed in the United States of America

FIRST EDITION

Library of Congress Cataloging-in-Publication Data

Anderson, Clifford.
   The stages of life: a groundbreaking discovery: the steps to psychological maturity/Clifford Anderson.—1st ed.
   Includes bibliographical references and index.
   ISBN 0-87113-481-0
   1. Maturation (Psychology) 2. Emotional maturity. 3. Developmental psychology. I. Title.
   BF710.A53 1995   155.2'5—dc20   94-43724

The Atlantic Monthly Press
841 Broadway
New York, NY 10003

10 9 8 7 6 5 4 3 2

to my children,

Nicholas, Brian, and Derek

Acknowledgments

*T*his book evolved in stages over a period of probably fifteen years. Although very few people participated in its creation, those who did made invaluable contributions.

Linda Miller has worked with me on this project for over a decade. Her contribution is impossible to overstate. She possesses not only a marvelous eye for detail but the combination of talent, temperament, brilliance, and tenacity to bring such a project to fruition.

Norman Lobsenz has worked on this project for more years than either of us cares to admit. His exceptional writing skills contributed mightily to this work.

David Holland read and then reread the text at several stages in its production. Through the years he provided a stream of valuable suggestions.

Selma Shapiro, Clyde Burleson, and Nancy Holland made valuable suggestions. Sam Vaughan was an early source of encouragement. The friendship of Dieter and Karin Scherfenberg deserves special mention.

My agent, John Diamond, called upon his extensive knowledge of the industry and found exactly the right publisher for this project.

~ Acknowledgments ~

Morgan Entrekin, my publisher and editor, saw from very little material the importance of placing these concepts in the public eye and instantly committed to the task. His personal interest was evident from the outset, and his traditional approach to publishing accommodated every unforeseen demand of the writing process.

It is the theory that decides what we can observe.

ALBERT EINSTEIN

Contents

~ Contents ~

The Stages of Life

Part I

~ 1 ~

A New Beginning

*T*his book sets forth a new theory of how a human being develops psychologically. Based on a set of startling new discoveries, it will show how each of us is exquisitely designed to move along an inner pathway that leads from birth to fully mature adulthood. As one might expect, then, this book will introduce many new ideas, new concepts. In essence, however, the book is not so much about concepts and ideas as it is about you as an individual. And about me. And about your family, your friends, your co-workers—indeed, it is about everyone you know.

It is about how we become the people we are. It is about gaining a vivid new understanding that will help us achieve a more complete and fulfilling life. It is about a very different way to perceive and understand the process of *psychological maturation*—a process in which, as you will see, we actively but unknowingly engage every day of our lives.

For almost a century now our ideas about psychological maturation have been based on bits and pieces of information taken from various theories. These fragments, recycled in a variety of ways, have until now been the only guides we have had to help us understand what is probably the single most important process occurring within us. This information has been crafted in many ways to help us avoid the hidden pitfalls of psychological development. It has been on such data that we have relied for our approaches to parenting, to education, to personal relationships, and to our own development. But the outcome of our endeavors in these areas has been inconsistent, confusing, and disappointing because the theories that guide us have proven vague and, worse yet, contradictory. Perhaps it is because of this that our society has gone through so many changes in its ideas about child rearing, schooling, family life, and intimate relationships.

Hence, it should come as no surprise that existing theory simply does not measure up to the job of helping us become psychologically mature. This leaves us to face the greater conflicts in our lives (and sometimes even the minor problems) with no clear understanding of what we are trying to achieve and how best to achieve it. Our theories leave us spending the first few decades of life attempting to accomplish a task we cannot yet even conceptualize correctly. In fact, our instincts are frequently better than our theories.

The centerpiece of this book is a revolutionary set of concepts I call *maturational theory*. This theory holds that the process of becoming psychologically mature rests solely on the ability to develop the mind correctly. It explains what happens in—and to—the mind during the process. And it explains how reaching a state of psychological maturity is the ultimate goal of an unconscious process that is built into our being.

As we see ourselves and those around us in this book, not only do we gain stunning insights into the process of our mental growth but, perhaps more important, we get a clearer understanding of why we behave as we do, why we find ourselves facing internal conflict, and how we develop the skills to resolve it.

By framing the process of psychological maturation from its inception at birth to its completion at full maturity, maturational theory makes it understandable and predictable. And by providing a "map," and a timetable, that outlines the structure and course of psychological development, this book enables us to fit ourselves into the process—to understand where we are on the maturational path, where we need to be, and what we need to do to get there.

Among other topics this book will explain:

- What "growing up" psychologically really means
- Why so many of our personal relationships fail
- What parenting is designed to accomplish
- Why our schools are failing our children
- What makes a person become "lost in" or overly dependent on a new hobby or interest—jogging or other fitness activities, a quest for spiritual knowledge, a search for individuality—which can be pursued so intensely that it replaces friendships and loving relationships
- Why some people cannot make a commitment to a job or a relationship, and why some cannot break away from an unsuitable job or a destructive relationship
- What the "midlife crisis" really is, and how in the long run it serves us well

This book does not merely provide explanations for these situations, behaviors, and processes; it also shows how to conceptualize these and other subjects in a way that promotes continued psychological development.

Beyond these "self-help" aspects, however, the book has two larger purposes: first, to set forth a general theory of psychological maturation—a primer, if you will—that provides an accurate and clear overview of an ongoing and real-time process within the developing mind, and, second, to open the pathway that makes real the immense potential for full maturity that exists in every person.

As a primer, this book presents the simplest model of the maturational process—highlighting its essential features without burdening the reader with all the parts. As an overview, it does not go into great detail but, instead, conveys a sense of the whole.

And one other note: The paradigm constructed in this book is the ideal paradigm of psychological development. It depicts what *should* happen during the growing-up process, *how* it should happen, and *when*.

Because maturational theory is new, we shall begin by looking at what has heretofore been available to help us understand how we develop psychologically.

~ 2 ~

The Search for a Valid Theory

Our understanding of how we become psychologically mature has developed slowly and erratically over time. For most of history, our ideas have been based largely on the concepts of *learning theory,* a theory that embraces the belief that psychological maturation occurs through the simple accumulation of everyday knowledge: The more knowledge one acquires and stores, the more mature one becomes.

Maturation According to Learning Theory

Under learning theory, immaturity is viewed as a state of deficiency. Children are seen as little adults who are not yet educated and are therefore incomplete. For them, becoming psychologically mature means filling in their missing pieces through the teaching/learning process. Once a child accumulates enough knowledge to function competently in the wider world, he or she is considered mature. Indeed, through the ages and across all cultures, the universal standard for psychological maturity has been threefold: the ability to work, to marry, and to assume the responsibility of rearing children.

Implicit in learning theory is the thesis that psychological growth takes place from the outside in—that is, most of the knowledge critical to the growing-up process originates in the external world. For parents, then, the central task is to select important information and pass it on to their children. The work of internalizing this information falls to the child—a process made easier by such characteristics as self-discipline, the ability to concentrate and focus, a good memory, and so on.

Not surprisingly, the more complex society becomes, the more knowledge there is to store, and the longer it takes to become psychologically mature. A century ago, children could learn enough to be considered mature by the time they reached puberty. Today most learning theorists would agree that such a goal is not achieved until the late teen years, or even the early twenties.

As a tool for understanding psychological maturation, learning theory is straightforward, clear, remarkably simple, and wrong. Yet it remained unchallenged until the turn of the twentieth century.

A Psychological Technique Leads to a Discovery

In the early 1890s, a young Viennese neurologist began experimenting with new approaches to the treatment of some common "neurological" problems. Sigmund Freud reasoned that these disorders were caused by problems within the mind; that is, they were psychological rather than physical in origin.[1] As such, he believed they might be amenable to cure through the use of purely psychological treatment.

Freud first tried hypnosis, with mixed results. By 1893 he was using a technique he called *free association* to probe the mind and treat the disorders. It was the combination of these two techniques—hypnosis followed by free association—that led Freud to his most significant discovery: the existence of unconscious psychological activity that influences behavior in everyday life. We now call such activity *dynamic unconscious functioning* or, more popularly, *the unconscious*.

The history of science tells us that extending our range of observation beyond the limits of everyday perception has always been critical to the advancement of scientific knowledge. And so it was that the development of special techniques able to access the unconscious accomplished for psychology what the microscope did for biology. It opened for exploration a previously unknown world, knowledge of which would greatly expand the understanding of our species.

At first, interest in the unconscious centered on its role in the formation of illness. Freud saw the unconscious as a seething cauldron of traumatic childhood memories, which occasionally would spill over into consciousness and cause disturbing, even crippling physical and psychological symptoms. He found that uncovering—and thereby releasing—these memories could end, or at least diminish, their devastating impact. Soon a small group of physicians was successfully using the free associative technique to relieve their patients of these dark memories. Thus the earliest phase of *psychoanalysis* was born.

As scientists continued to probe the unconscious, their work led to a second and more far-reaching discovery: Certain psychological abilities, once thought to be the consequence of a conscious teaching/learning process, actually seemed to emerge from a gradually unfolding unconscious process. We now know that some of these abilities form the basis for cognitive skills such as the abilities to count, to tell time, and to determine size, shape, and volume. Another group of abilities enables us to form and enrich personal and social relationships. Bonding, sharing, coupling, caring, and committing fall into this category, as do emotional abilities such as loving, and experiencing pride, shame, or guilt. Behavioral scientists generally agree that together, cognitive and relationship abilities form the psychological basis for understanding and engaging in the world.[2]

Discovering this unconscious process, named the *developmental process,* caused many scientists to reframe their understanding of psychological maturation. They discarded the outside-in model of learning theory in favor of the inside-out developmental model. This shift reoriented scientific thinking. And it may prove to have been as important to understanding the design of psychological maturation as the Copernican shift (from an earth-centered to a sun-centered model of our solar system) was to understanding the design of the universe.

Developmental Theory

Theory that tells us about this unconscious process and its contribution to the life of a maturing person is called *developmental theory.* Today, developmental theory reigns as the explanation for how we grow up psychologically. To summarize it briefly, developmental theory holds that psychological maturation originates within the unconscious through the establishment of independent *psychological abilities.* Each ability, emerging from a gradually unfolding internal process, functions as a step on the path to psychological maturity. The more the process unfolds, the greater the number of abilities established and the more mature the person becomes.

But as behavioral scientists continued to focus on their explorations of this process, they soon noted a curious characteristic. There seemed to be no assurance—no guarantee, if you will—that any or all of these abilities would be established. Hence, they concluded that psychological maturity is not an automatic outcome of the growing-up process.

Unlike in physical maturation, which can virtually be taken for granted in most youngsters, newly emerging psychological abilities must be nurtured if psychological maturation is to proceed correctly. Moreover, if that nurture is lacking, the resulting development could be flawed, or compromised. Limited compromise could result in minor psychological impairment; more substantial compromise might well bring the entire developmental process to a halt—a phenomenon known as *developmental arrest.*

This new knowledge—that the developmental process must be nurtured if it is to flower—changed most traditional approaches to child rearing. Instead of teaching a child to be mature, enlightened parents shifted their focus to fostering this unfolding, unconscious process. And because intellectual development is believed to flow from the same process, nurturing a child's psychological development became the central task of teachers and others in the educational arena.

Clues to a Hidden Developmental Process

Yet how can one nurture a process buried deep within an unconscious core? According to developmental theory, the answer lies in understanding a unique characteristic of the developmental process: Not all aspects of psychological development are concealed. Some newly developing abilities are "practiced" before they become securely established. And this practicing phase of the developmental process can be observed in everyday behavior.

Let's look at an example of *practicing behavior*. At about eighteen months, a child develops the ability to say no. But first the child practices this behavior by saying no to virtually everything and everyone. Once the child finally "understands" how to say no—in other words, when the practicing has "worked" and the ability is firmly established—the need to practice abruptly ceases. Not surprisingly, the appearance—and then sudden disappearance—of various practicing behaviors is largely responsible for creating the many "phases" one passes through during the growing-up process.

We now know that responding correctly to practicing behavior nurtures correct development. Failing to do so puts newly emerging steps at risk and increases the possibility of compromising the formation of essential psychological abilities.

Consider this example. Adam, a two-year-old, refuses to eat peas and carrots. Under the sway of learning theory, this child would be seen as being disobedient. Good parenting, then, would dictate that the child be taught to obey. In earlier eras, Adam might have been firmly strapped into a specially designed chair, allowing his parents to leave the table while Adam contemplated the merits of eating peas and carrots.

However, we now understand from developmental theory that at Adam's age (known to parents as the "terrible twos") refusing to eat peas and carrots most likely represents an attempt to develop what psychologists call a sense of autonomy. We also know that oppositionality as practicing behavior is to be tolerated, even encouraged, because it promotes psychological development. Instead of forcing the issue, enlightened parents can offer the child an assortment of vegetables; Adam might still say no to peas and carrots but choose to eat green beans. His parents are pleased because not only are they meeting his nutritional needs, but, more important, by correctly responding to practicing behavior, they have nurtured and therefore facilitated Adam's underlying developmental process.

It is often difficult to identify practicing behavior. To help the layperson recognize it, psychologists and psychiatrists have constructed developmental maps, which identify known forms of practicing behavior (for example, oppositionality in the two-year-old) and then match them with the corresponding newly emerging abilities (in this case, those integral to developing a sense of autonomy). Such maps also frequently suggest responses that will help promote psychological growth—for instance, offering alternatives (to peas and carrots), or, in other situations, ignoring behavior, redirecting a child's attention, and so on.

Maps enable us to look at ourselves, our children, students, friends, and others, and place many practicing behaviors in developmental perspective. The information in such maps is available from a variety of sources, ranging from pediatricians to psychotherapists; from television talk shows to magazine articles and newspaper advice columns; from support groups to books on education, parenting, and personal development. All are useful to some degree, because being able to place practicing behavior in developmental perspective helps us offer the kind of nurturing responses that are essential to both correct development and sustained psychological growth.

Consider the example of sixteen-year-old Julie, who wants to quit school and marry her boyfriend. From our developmental maps, we know that most adolescent "love" cannot be taken at face value. It is more likely to be a type of practicing behavior that reflects an attempt to develop the psychological capacity to couple romantically. But Julie feels only the emotional rush of what she thinks is everlasting love, along with the desire to quit school and move forward in life with a new husband. Julie's parents, by contrast, are able to place her behavior in developmental perspective. They know, as a general rule, that commitments made as part of a developmental phase can rarely be sustained permanently. Or, even worse, that it is possible for such premature commitments to derail the developmental process. Her parents also know that in a short time Julie's feelings for this young man most probably will change and that this phase in her growing-up process will be replaced by the next. In this illustration, Julie's parents understand—on the basis of the maps available to them—that they can best ensure their daughter's continued psychological growth by dissuading her from marrying her boyfriend.

An Unfulfilled Promise

The discovery of an unfolding unconscious process brought enormous promise. For if scientists could catalog newly emerging abilities and their attendant principles of development, could they not then determine other critical aspects of the developmental process? Perhaps even its fundamental design? And once we knew that design, could we not more easily and completely meet the requirements of psychological development? Such knowledge would be analogous to the modeling developed in, say, chemistry over the past two centuries. Working from a list of basic elements, chemists first were able to determine how molecules and more complex structures are formed and then to understand the internal structure of material along with the principles and conditions that permit it to form. With these essential elements of design in place, chemists were ultimately able to devise methods for creating new and useful materials.

By the same token, developmental modeling could turn the seemingly helter-skelter process of growing up into more of a science. Behaviorists could create specific profiles of each phase of the developmental process, providing us with an accurate understanding of the changes that occur throughout psychological immaturity. Parents, teachers, and therapists, now able to perceive accurately the path of psychological maturation, could easily recognize practicing behaviors and then respond in ways that would best nurture the growing-up process.

But these potentials have been achieved only to a limited degree. It is true, for example, that experts in developmental theory can isolate many newly emerging psychological abilities. They can confidently postulate that the capacity to function emotionally and intellectually emerges one step at a time out of the unfolding developmental process. And they have identified many forms of practicing behavior and correlated them with the formation of specific unconscious developmental steps. In so doing, they have provided us with valuable guidance that enhances parenting skills, makes education more effective, makes psychotherapy more efficient, and facilitates self-development.

But as important and useful as developmental theory has been, it, like learning theory, is flawed. And the full promise seemingly inherent in this theory has never been realized.

To begin with, despite the various techniques available to them for probing the unconscious, behavioral scientists have never been able to isolate an actual unfolding developmental process. Each investigatory technique they use isolates merely a different set of developing abilities. And each set of abilities suggests a somewhat different unconscious developmental pattern. All attempts to combine the various patterns into a single coherent design have failed. In truth, there are now about as many theories of psychological development as there are theoreticians.[3]

A second problem with developmental theory is that although the various techniques used to access unconscious functioning do reveal the progressive establishment of steps through adolescence, all evidence of an unfolding sequence ends there. The profile of psychological maturation outlined by developmental theory (as an unfolding sequence of emerging abilities) simply fizzles out at this early point in the life cycle. As a result, we naturally assume that psychological immaturity comes to a close in the late teens.[4] It is also assumed that any future development is merely the consequence of combining and enriching already existing abilities, rather than a continued unfolding of new abilities.[5]

These assumptions raise several questions. Do new psychological abilities really stop emerging with the end of adolescence? And if so, does that mean the underlying developmental process is complete? Or is it possible that new abilities continue to unfold into youth and adulthood but go undetected by our current techniques?

These are enormously important questions. As we have seen, the capacity to isolate elements of an unfolding process is what enables scientists to identify practicing behaviors. And being aware of practicing behavior is what enables us to nurture the developmental process, which, in turn, helps stimulate correct development. Moreover, knowledge of an unfolding process puts developmental phases in perspective, enabling a maturing person to make better life decisions. For instance, most people would agree with Julie's parents that the urge to marry at sixteen is an example of practicing behavior and part of a temporary developmental phase. Therefore, life decisions such as marriage and childbearing are normally discouraged for adolescents.

But what about the desire to marry at age eighteen, or twenty, or twenty-five? Why isn't the broken marriage of a thirty-year-old couple—failed because they have "grown in different directions''—also seen as the logical consequence of a commitment made while still in the throes of a developmental phase?

Because developmental theory has been unable to isolate a continuing unconscious developmental sequence beyond adolescence, we have come to believe that adult behavior is no longer phasic, that it can comfortably be taken at face value. Thus, when Julie comes home at twenty-five years of age with a young man she wants to marry, her parents are delighted (or at least accepting). They believe she has reached an age where she is mature enough to make her own decisions about a lifelong commitment. Any concerns the parents may have at this point are more likely to be based on factors such as the young man's character, or his earning potential, the couple's compatibility, and so on. And when Julie's marriage ends a few years later in divorce, as so many do, it is invariably viewed as some sort of failing or mistake, rather than as the logical consequence of a commitment made while in the midst of yet another developmental phase.

Still another limitation of developmental theory is that it offers no clear description of the basic nature of psychological maturity. If psychological development is achieved through the establishment of individual abilities, then surely at some point these abilities come together in some configuration—some structure or system—we can recognize as the end point to the immature phase of the life cycle and the beginning of psychological maturity. But developmental theorists have not found any such end point. Like learning theory, developmental theory subscribes to what may be called the "rule of sufficiency": When sufficient development/learning exists for a person to engage competently in the world, that person is deemed mature. This definition, based solely on socially desirable characteristics, substitutes for a definition based on a specific configuration of unconscious psychological abilities. At best, this is a limited way to think about psychological maturity, somewhat analogous to defining a diamond solely on the basis of its hardness.

Finally, in the greater scheme of things, developmental theory is limited by its inability to isolate what is developing within the person. Is it the ego? The mind? The "self"? In other words, if psychological abilities are the parts, what exactly is the "whole"? Different developmental theories point to different conclusions. In truth, no one seems to know.

Yet correctly understanding the fundamental nature of a whole subject or system is a central problem in every branch of science. Professor Alan Lightman, of the Massachusetts Institute of Technology, explains this as the need to view a subject from the outside:

> A universal feature of knowledge is that one must get outside of a thing to understand it. To understand the crucial aspect of an airplane, one must stand on the ground and watch it move through the air overhead; an understanding of the essentials of American society required the visit of Alexis de Tocqueville from France; a famous theorem of mathematics, Gödel's theorem, says that the truth or falsity of certain statements in each branch of mathematics cannot be ascertained without going beyond that branch to another area of mathematics.[6]

All in all, I am suggesting that developmental theory is merely a collection of nebulous and frequently incompatible ideas. While some individual theories may have substantial usefulness, all are riddled with inherent problems. Yet developmental theory remains the only viable general theory of psychological maturation in existence. It is all we have to define our understanding of immaturity and maturity, and it is all we have to provide us with the theoretical underpinnings used in parenting, education, self-development, and psychotherapy.

I believe the problems with developmental theory exist because the techniques used to create the theory only partially reveal the unconscious process of development. This limitation leads to a sort of "blind men and the elephant" predicament, in which each man believed the part of the creature he was touching represented the whole animal. In developmental theory, similarly, a few scattered observations have led to a distorted portrait of the entire process of psychological maturation.

A New Theory of Psychological Maturation

This book sets forth a completely new model of the developmental process. It took shape and substance out of scores of observations accumulated through the use of a newly discovered technique for probing the unconscious. And it is remarkably different from the models crafted by developmental and learning theory. This new model, created from *maturational theory,* enables us to view "from the outside" both the unfolding unconscious process and the subsequent achievement of psychological maturity. Maturational theory thus creates an understanding of psychological maturation from the perspective of the whole.

This view readily confirms two postulates of developmental theory: that psychological maturation is the consequence of the establishment of new abilities; and that these abilities emerge from a gradually unfolding, unconscious process. At this point, however, maturational theory reaches beyond developmental theory to reveal the grander design of the process as well as its ultimate purpose.

Maturational theory holds that the process of psychological maturation is designed to construct the system the mind uses to create its fundamental understanding of the world. It also holds that only when this system is complete is the mind capable of creating a fully correct understanding of the world. And only then is a person truly mature.

Maturational Theory: An Early Overview

The mind at birth is in a primitive, undifferentiated state, unable to build even the most elementary understanding of the world. According to maturational theory, it will require some three decades of nearly continuous development for the mind to establish enough psychological abilities to construct a fully correct understanding of the world. This means that the formation of newly emerging abilities does not end with the termination of adolescence, as stated in developmental theory. Rather, new abilities continue to develop up to and through the middle years of life. Indeed, maturational theory holds that what we are now calling the midlife crisis is what actually marks the transition from immaturity to maturity. And, as a matter of course, this period of transition should normally occur in one's late twenties or early thirties. Maturational theory also holds that:

- Practicing behavior continues throughout immaturity. This means that behaviors in the midtwenties, such as getting married or divorced, having children, and so on, may reflect attempts to facilitate psychological maturation. Further, maturational theory states that many other behaviors that occur today in the twenties and even the thirties and forties—such as sexual behaviors, social alienation, running and other forms of physical fitness, the search for individuality, and the behaviors of the midlife crisis—are in many cases practicing behaviors that reflect ongoing development. And as with the practicing behaviors of childhood and adolescence, placing these in developmental perspective facilitates nurturing of the unfolding developmental process, which, in turn, stimulates correct development.

- The mature mind is established in an easily recognizable configuration, which serves as a clear basis for defining the state of psychological maturity.
- The limitations of learning and developmental theory are a product of the techniques used to access the unconscious as well as the linguistic structure of the theories themselves—subjects that will be explored later.
- Moreover, unlike its predecessors—developmental theory and learning theory—maturational theory allows every aspect of psychological development to be brought under one roof, so to speak.

But in order to conceptualize fully the scope of these discoveries, one must first understand the technique that led to the creation of this new theory.

~ 3 ~

Exploring the Unconscious

Since Freud's discovery of the unconscious a century ago, our understanding of psychological maturation has proceeded in a slow and uneven manner. While remarkable progress has been made in some areas, virtually none has been made in others. Compared with the giant steps taken in that same hundred-year period in the "hard" sciences—physics, biology, chemistry—it is as if our grasp of the developmental process has remained immobilized in its infancy, barely able to creep.

What accounts for the disparity in the rates of discovery? I believe the primary obstacle to understanding the growing-up process is rooted in the characteristics of the unconscious and the tools available to us to access it.

Reaching into the Unconscious

Because psychological maturation is a product of unconscious functioning—which by definition is inaccessible to everyday experience—whoever would explore the growing-up process must somehow find a way to reach into the uncon-

23

scious and then identify and isolate those elements within it that affect psychological maturation. But what tools can behavioral scientists use to do this? Researchers in the hard sciences have a wealth of devices they can use to observe their subjects: Astronomers have telescopes, biologists have electron microscopes, physicists have particle accelerators. Behavioral scientists have no such "hard-wired" instruments. Instead, for the better part of this century, psychologists have relied on various "intellectual" techniques to seek out clues to the nature of the unconscious.

Outside-in Techniques

Although many such techniques are available today, all of them enable scientists to access unconscious functioning in only one of two ways. The most commonly used approach starts "on the surface," with a specific psychological skill to be studied. Then, choosing one or more available techniques, the observer tries to identify the unconscious process leading to creation of the skill.

Say a psychologist is interested in determining the origin of a child's capacity to form friendships. Techniques available for this study might include play therapy, projective testing, and/or observation over an extended period of time (longitudinal study). Other skills that might be studied in this manner include simple language abilities, such as early verbal skills, or simple numerical skills, such as counting from one to ten. They might also be complex: abstract thinking, or adolescent independence—skills built from many individual steps over the course of psychological maturation.

Once a skill along with its unconscious origin or origins is isolated, studied, and understood, this "complex" functions as a single piece in the overall developmental process. Then, much as one would assemble a jigsaw puzzle, scientists construct their models of psychological maturation.

But all these techniques, because they begin at the surface, severely restrict access to unconscious functioning. They preclude the scientist from making the wider range of observations required to identify all the processes involved in establishing a given skill. And the developmental profiles resulting from these techniques reflect this limitation: They convey only a patchwork pattern of psychological skills with more or less clouded unconscious origins.

An Inside-out Technique

A second approach to accessing the unconscious begins "on the inside," using special techniques that can bypass everyday behavior and peer directly at psychological functioning. By far the best example in this category is the psychoanalytic technique of *free association*. If Freud's greatest achievement was the discovery of the unconscious, then arguably his second greatest was the development of the free associative technique.

In the psychoanalytic setting, a patient—usually an adult, occasionally an adolescent—is asked to say whatever comes to mind. What follows is a progressive but manageable loss of *psychological stability*. As *instability* sets in, the patient automatically moves to develop those psychological abilities that will return the mind to the stable position. Sometimes this means creating entirely new abilities. Other times it means redeveloping psychological abilities, which, although already formed, were formed incorrectly. In either case, it is the need to restabilize the mind that actually stimulates psychological development.

But in the analytic process, the pressure of continuing free association causes any newfound stability to quickly collapse. The resulting instability fosters additional development. Over time this repetitive cycle—stability, free association, instability, psychological development, and a return to stability—assumes the characteristics of an unfolding process. The psychoanalyst's observations of this process form the database for various theories about the greater developmental process.

But this approach is also limited when it comes to discerning our basic maturational design. For although the free associative technique provides greatly expanded access to unconscious functioning, it uncovers psychological steps laid down mainly in the first few years of life. More specifically, it produces little more than the sequence of steps that must be reworked to cure the neurosis that brought the patient "to the couch" in the first place. Thus, classic free association yields only a partial inventory of mostly early-forming abilities. That is why the attempt to build a comprehensive developmental theory from psychoanalytic observations has not proved successful. And it is why psychoanalytic developmental theory itself has been partly responsible for our current, incorrect understanding of psychological maturation.

A New Psychoanalytic Technique

As a psychoanalyst I, too, have spent thousands of hours using the free associative technique with my patients, observing the results. In the course of my work I found that the psychoanalytic process stimulated the development of two distinct types of psychological abilities, which I named *type-1* and *type-2*.[1]

Type-1 abilities seemed to emerge spontaneously and unexpectedly from deep within the unconscious core. Patients would be free-associating, saying whatever came to mind, when without warning they would have seemingly unrelated insights or revelations. For example, while free-associating, one patient unexpectedly said, "I can say no." The type-1 ability that enabled him unconditionally to say no had just redeveloped in uncompromised form. Another patient was free-associating when the insight occurred to her that a troubling set of interactions between close friends had nothing to do with her. In this case, the capacity to conceptualize independent action had just developed—a psychological ability that normally should first appear at about age five or six.

I came to believe that, for whatever reason, only type-1 abilities are central to the ongoing process of psychological maturation. Acting on this belief, I decided to alter the traditional free associative technique to facilitate their development, treating type-2 ability development as incidental or as clutter. (We shall return to type-1 and type-2 abilities later.)

Centering a psychoanalytic technique on only type-1 ability formation turned out to be a major undertaking. Ordinarily, forty-five minutes to an hour is set aside for each analytic session. But ideally this new technique calls for free-associating continuously until the next type-1 ability is created. This might require an hour, but it could require from several hours to an entire day. Moreover, in classic psychoanalysis a patient attends three to five analytic sessions each week. What I have come to call *maturationally based free association* needs to be undertaken seven days a week, every week of the year.

Also, in traditional psychoanalysis, patients free-associate in the presence of a psychoanalyst, who guides them through the traps of the psychoanalytic process. But the exorbitant time demand of maturationally based free association would mean giving up the conventional session in the presence of the analyst. Because it was not feasible to ask any of my patients to embark on such a time-consuming and experimental project, I decided, for better or worse, to set out on this path alone—to free-associate by myself, unassisted.

Free-associating now meant saying whatever came to mind until the next type-1 ability formed, then repeating the sequence. Simply following the development of each type-1 ability had the effect of releasing me from the influence of all existing psychological theory, because I was driven only by the pursuit of the next type-1 ability. There were no preconceived notions—no expectations other than those created by my intuitive sense that ultimately this track, although unorthodox, would prove beneficial.

Building a Model

With this plan in hand, I spent many hours over the next several years free-associating, forming within myself a substantial number of type-1 abilities. These abilities invariably seemed to function as psychological actions that enabled my mind to perform old tasks in new ways, or to perform altogether new tasks. For example, in childhood I, like most children, had developed the psychological abilities to grasp and to let go of. But for whatever reason, these abilities had been compromised during their formation. To be corrected, each needed to be redeveloped during the free associative process.[2]

Other abilities, such as the ability to tolerate a void and the ability to follow an intuitively based path, probably developed for the first time. These abilities are associated with more advanced forms of psychological functioning, and with proper development, they should appear during the third decade of life. At any rate, the net effect of my type-1 ability development was that my mind was undergoing noticeable change. I felt as if it were advancing—maturing, if you will.

From early on, I recorded each developing ability, along with any steps or events I believed led to its formation. And because, during free association, abilities seem to develop (or redevelop) in random order, I had to reorder these abilities into the probable sequence in which they would have naturally unfolded (a practice well established in classic psychoanalytic theory formation). Reconstructing the natural sequence enabled me to understand how each new ability, functioning with others that had already formed, enhanced psychological functioning.

After some 20,000 hours of free association, it became clear that the wide array of abilities I had cataloged all functioned with one common purpose: to construct the system the mind uses to create a fundamental understanding of the world.[3]

Over approximately 30,000 hours of free association, enough type-1 abilities had developed for me to determine the basic design of this system. Understanding the design then enabled me to take the final step: to portray this design in a life cycle model that clearly and simply conveys the essence of the growing-up process—a process through which, I believe, each of us can become psychologically mature.

~ 4 ~

Psychological Maturation:
Two Models

Not possessing divine knowledge, we human beings must create an understanding of the world from scratch. We do this by amassing information gleaned through our various senses. This information is then shaped into models, which become the carriers of what we know—the templates we use to understand and develop our world.

Humankind, in short, is a model-dependent species. We know, for example, that the earth is round and orbits about the sun. How do we know that? Certainly not because it appears so. We know it because astronomers have created this model, which we accept as correct. (Of course in an earlier era people accepted a model of an earth-centered system; increased knowledge, therefore, can change incorrect models into correct ones.) Science abounds in models: $E = mc^2$, for example; the twin helixes of DNA; opposite magnetic poles attract, like poles repel. But models can convey more than scientific information. We use some models to help us grasp political, social, economic, and religious concepts. The concept of capitalism or socialism models an entire governmental structure.

And we use some models to guide us in our life decisions.

An education model that tells us that the more education we get the more money we are likely to earn spurs students to seek a college education as the key to financial success. Television commercials model body images which purport to tell us that a pretty face or a slender figure is the key to romantic success. And parents, consciously or not, model values for their children.

A model, in short, can be defined as a compact representation of a fact, a concept, or a feeling. It condenses large amounts of information into a manageable form that enables us to grasp a given subject more easily. At heart, all science is the pursuit of models that reliably depict the world we live in. The more accurate and reliable the model, the more advanced the science.

Interestingly enough, most scientists today would probably agree that there are few reliable models in the behavioral sciences—with one exception. For the past century developmental theorists have taken as axiomatic the profile of how we grow up psychologically. That is, the life cycle is divided into two phases—immaturity and maturity. Immaturity encompasses childhood and adolescence; maturity is synonymous with adulthood.

This is called a *life cycle model,* and in the behavioral sciences life cycle models are very important. For one thing, they establish a framework that enables us to see complex patterns of growth and development that occur naturally over the life span—for example, the framework of childhood, adolescence, and adulthood; or, of immaturity and maturity. Also, life cycle models highlight the patterns and milestones associated with the process of becoming psychologically mature—for example, oppositionality in the two-year-old, rebelliousness during adolescence, the onset of adulthood. Understanding these patterns influences the way we live our lives: the way we parent and educate our children;

the personal choices we make and the time frame in which we make them.

The Life Cycle Model of Developmental Theory

Based on developmental theory, our current model of psychological maturation holds that it takes merely the better part of two decades to become mature; by the early twenties, the newly mature adult is supposedly positioned to understand and engage in the world competently. (This life cycle model is what guided Julie's parents when they dissuaded her from marrying when she was only sixteen years old; the same model guided them again when they accepted her decision to marry at twenty-five.) The remaining course of one's life, developmental theory says, is determined primarily by such variables as education, talent, and opportunity, as well as by such personal characteristics as perseverance and the willingness to work. These tenets define the framework of immaturity and maturity as it shapes our overall understanding of the human life cycle. And over the years this basic framework has had only one generally accepted addition to its profile.

Not quite forty years ago, the psychoanalyst Erik Erikson noticed that the later years of adolescence were beset by increased turbulence and instability. Parents often label this period adolescent "searching," but Erikson saw it as a time when adolescents are struggling to form and solidify a sense of who they are. He labeled this period the *identity crisis* because the turbulence and instability dissipated upon the establishment of an inner sense of identity.[1]

Erikson thus saw the identity crisis as a normal developmental crisis—that is, a natural, built-in period of struggle and growth during a specific phase of the developmental process. Today, most behavioral scientists agree that crisis periods are legitimate components of the life cycle, and that the identity crisis specifically signals the transformation from adolescence to adulthood—from psychological immaturity to psychological maturity. (See Figure 1.)

Life Phase:	*Immaturity*		*Maturity*
Life Stage:	Childhood	Adolescence	Adulthood
Life Crisis:		Identity	
Age:	0	10	20

Erik Erikson's Life Cycle Model
FIGURE 1

This profile was briefly challenged in 1970 by the Yale University psychologist Kenneth Keniston. In a paper titled "Youth: A 'New' Stage of Life," Keniston suggested that the decade of the 1960s had seen a "new" stage of life emerge into the general population. He called it "youth" and positioned it between adolescence and adulthood. The life cycle model was now childhood, adolescence, then youth, and finally adulthood.[2]

Moreover, suggested Keniston, each life stage could be characterized and defined by a newly developed type of thinking. *Childhood* is defined by *concrete* or literal *thinking*. The development of the added capacity to think *abstractly*— that is, to engage in hypothetical and deductive reasoning— signals the onset of movement into *adolescence*.

Keniston amplified the purely psychological underpinnings of these stage-of-life designations by pointing out that being a teenager and being an adolescent are frequently not synonymous.[3] By definition, he said, everyone between the ages of thirteen and nineteen is a teenager, but only teenagers who have developed the capacity to think abstractly can truly be considered to be in the adolescent life stage. Teenagers who are still limited to concrete thinking have become developmentally arrested, stuck in the childhood stage of life. Keniston suggested the term *pseudoadolescent* to designate such a teenager.

Keniston considered *youth* an optional stage of life. That is, he said, one can become mature without going through it. But if it emerges, it does so in the late teenage years, hand in hand with the development of the capacity to think *relativistically*. He viewed the relativistic thinker as a person who can conceptualize issues from diverse perspectives, or frames of reference. For example, someone is in youth when he or she is able to consider an issue from an unfamiliar or distant vantage, such as the viewpoint of another person. (The capacity for relativistic thinking later becomes an integral part of gender, social, cultural, historical, and political awareness.)

Keniston did not suggest an underlying cognitive characteristic for adulthood; he merely moved that stage of life a little further upstream, so to speak, from the end of the second to roughly the middle of the third decade of life.[4] This made room for the stage of youth to be inserted into his life cycle model.

Keniston had now amended the traditional concept of psychological maturation in three ways. First, he inserted youth as the third stage of life. Next, he extended immaturity from the late teens into the early or midtwenties. And third, he proposed cognitive definitions for all three immature life stages. In so doing, he severed the ties between life stages and specific age frames and instead tied life stages to a testable form of cognitive development. (See Figure 2.)

Life Phase:	Immaturity			Maturity
Life Stage:	Childhood	Adolescence	Youth	Adulthood
Defining Cognitive Characteristic:	Concrete	Abstract	Relativistic	None
Age	0	10	20	25

Kenneth Keniston's Life Cycle Model
FIGURE 2

Keniston's treatment of youth as a stage of life ultimately departed completely from developmental theory when he said youth was of social as well as psychological origin. He wrote:

> To explain how it is possible for "new" stages of life to emerge under changed historical conditions would require a lengthy excursion into the theory of psychological development. It should suffice here to emphasize that the direction and extent of human development—indeed the entire nature of the human life cycle—is by no means predetermined by man's biological constitution. Instead, psychological development results from a complex interplay of constitutional givens (including the rates and phases of biological maturation) and the changing familial, social, educational, economic, and political conditions that constitute the matrix in which children develop.[5]

A newly emerging stage of life was a provocative idea, but from the point of view of developmental theory it was sadly lacking. To accept youth as a legitimate stage of life, behavioral scientists would have had to verify an unfolding developmental process beyond adolescence. Because their techniques did not enable them to do this, Keniston's work could not be supported, leaving his model as fascinating conjecture with little inherent staying power.

Today, few are familiar with Keniston's work. However, I believe that many of his observations are valid—that he did indeed discover a newly emerging stage of life, and that he was right when he stated that immaturity can extend beyond adolescence. But I suggest that the lack of a better technique for observing unconscious behavior led Keniston to the wrong reason for the origin of the life stage he so perceptively discovered. Youth is not of psychosocial origin; rather, it is the manifestation of an ongoing unconscious psychological process.

A New Life Cycle Model

Like developmental theory, maturational theory postulates a life cycle composed of an immature and a mature phase. It also divides immaturity into three stages: childhood, adolescence, and youth. Maturity remains synonymous with adulthood.

But in contrast to Keniston's work and the classic models of developmental theory, maturational theory holds three other premises: (1) that youth is an essential, not an optional, stage of life—that is, one *must* pass through youth to become truly psychologically mature; (2) that the insertion of youth as a life stage delays the onset of adulthood—and maturity—beyond one's twenties and into one's early thirties; and (3) that what we now call the *midlife crisis* is actually the last in a series of normal developmental crises, signaling the transition from youth to adulthood—from immaturity to maturity.

Like Keniston, I believe that each immature stage of life is best defined by the establishment of a new type of thinking— childhood by concrete thinking, adolescence by abstract thinking, and youth by relativistic thinking. Maturational theory, however, identifies a special form of relativistic thinking, which develops in late youth. It enables the mind to place a topic within a broadened area or field rather than viewing it from a simple or discrete position. This means a topic can be put in context, thereby creating additional perspective. Hence it is called *contextual thinking* (see Figure 3).

Life Phase:	Immaturity			Maturity
Life Stage:	Childhood	Adolescence	Youth	Adulthood
Life Crisis:			Identity	Midlife
Defining Cognitive Characteristic:	Concrete	Abstract	Relativistic (Simple → Contextual)	
Age	0	10	20	30

Maturational Theory: Life Cycle Model
from the Perspective of How the Mind Thinks
FIGURE 3

At this point, the model of maturational theory departs from all other life cycle models and depicts psychological maturation from a completely different frame of reference: not primarily whether the mind "thinks" concretely, abstractly, or relativistically, and not whether a person is "responsible" enough to have a career and family. Rather, maturational theory views becoming mature in terms of how the mind constructs and completes a system that will determine how it understands the world.

Until now this crucial component of the life cycle model has been missing. This is analogous to telling the story of our solar system without mentioning the sun. As a consequence, even though children and adolescents spend the better portion of every day developing their minds psychologically, not once in all their years of formal education are they taught what they are unconsciously striving to accomplish. This puts our youngsters at serious disadvantage, considering that understanding the process of psychological maturation greatly facilitates accomplishing the process correctly.

And our youngsters are not the only disadvantaged. In the United States alone there are an estimated 30 to 50 million people in their twenties, thirties, and older who, I submit, are actively struggling with their development. Again, few if any of them are able to place the elements of their struggle in a context that allows them to understand what they are trying to accomplish. Yet many of them seem to know, on some level, that some force—some process—is driving the behavior that often surprises and dismays them.

Because the life cycle model of maturational theory creates a framework that accurately portrays this process, let us, for the moment, set aside the models of Erikson and Keniston and focus only on the progressive construction of the mature mind.

The Life Cycle Model of Maturational Theory: Constructing the Mind's Capacity to Understand

As stated earlier, the mind at birth is incapable of creating even the most elementary understanding of the world. According to maturational theory, it will take some three decades of nearly continuous type-1 ability development for the mind to complete its task of creating the means to understand the world.

This monumental accomplishment can be broken down into three phases. In the first phase, the mind constructs its capacity to access input relayed to the brain mostly from the first five (perceptual) senses. It uses this input to create a stable *interim understanding* of the world. During the second phase, still using mostly perceptual input, the mind systematically expands that portion of the world it can comprehend and deal with. And finally, during the third phase, the mind constructs the added capacity to utilize input from the sixth sense, intuition. With this step, the mind is positioned to create a fully correct understanding of the world.[6]

(I want to state here that in maturational theory the definition of *intuition* is quite specific and at odds with one of the most commonly used meanings of that word—to guess or to surmise. Suffice it to say that, psychologically, intuition enables the mind unconsciously to experience the *dynamic dimension* of a subject, just as, say, the sense of sight enables the mind to determine the appearance of a subject, or the sense of touch enables the mind to determine how something feels. This admittedly vague explanation will be expanded on later. For now, though, the important point is that intuition, as used in maturational theory, refers to a crucial form of input the mind needs to create a fully correct understanding of the extended world.)

The life cycle model of maturational theory showing the relationship between sensory input and types of understanding is depicted in Figure 4.

Type of Understanding:		Stable Interim	Fully Correct
Number of Senses:		Five	Six
Age	0	5	30

Maturational Theory: Life Cycle Model
Relationship Between Types of Understanding and
Sensory Input
FIGURE 4

This simple but inclusive model changes the way we think about growing up. Instead of thinking of maturing primarily in terms of events—relationships with parents, schooling, friendships, dating, graduating, becoming independent and leaving home—we view growing up as the process of developing the mind's capacity to understand the world.

From this frame of reference we now look at how the mind develops, one step at a time; what we can do to help develop the mind correctly; how the mind constructs its capacity to create an interim understanding of the world; what creating an interim understanding means; how the mind stabilizes itself; how the person is affected if the mind remains unstable or loses stability; how we can generally facilitate the process of becoming mature; and how becoming mature changes one's life.

Putting It All Together:
Three Stages of Life + Three Crises = Adulthood

Thinking about the life cycle as a sequence of psychological steps the mind takes along a *maturational path* creates a broader approach to understanding the growing-up process. From this new perspective, the stages of life during immaturity represent not only different levels of advancement in how the mind thinks—concretely in childhood, abstractly in adolescence, and relativistically in youth—but also the kind of input the mind accesses to create its understanding of the world: five senses or all six senses. According to maturational theory, the mind in childhood, adolescence, and youth uses input primarily from the first five senses to understand the world. Adulthood begins when the mind has constructed the stable capacity to create this understanding through the use of all six senses.[7]

One can now insert into this life cycle model the periods of normal *developmental crisis.* In life cycle terms, a period of crisis occurs whenever rapid transformations within the developing mind cause protracted turbulence and psychological instability. During immaturity, there are three periods of normal crisis (each of which will be examined in more detail later). The *Oedipal crisis* occurs at about age five, as the mind of early childhood takes the difficult final steps in constructing a stable interim capacity to understand the world. The *identity crisis* marks the transition from adolescence to youth. During this time, the mind undergoes an enormous expansion in its capacity to experience the world. What we now call the *midlife crisis* is the last normal developmental crisis. It occurs as the mind develops the type-1 abilities required to process input from the sixth sense, intuition. Completing this task successfully resolves the midlife crisis and signals the transition from youth to adulthood—from immaturity to maturity. (See Figure 5.)

Life Phase:	Immaturity			Maturity
Life Stage:	Childhood	Adolescence	Youth	Adulthood
Life Crisis:	Oedipal		Identity	Midlife
Defining Cognitive Characteristic:	Concrete	Abstract	Relativistic (Simple → Contextual)	
Number of Senses:	Five			Six
Type of Understanding:		Interim		Fully Correct
Age	0	10	20	30

Maturational Theory: Comprehensive Life Cycle Model
FIGURE 5

The Next Step

Even though the life cycle model historically has been familiar and popular, it is only a general psychological map. While it presents a broad overview of psychological development, it does little to fill in the specifics. It is fair to say that trying to understand psychological maturation through only a life cycle model—even a correct one—is somewhat similar to trying to understand the world with only a globe. A globe gives us the general layout of the land, from which we can get our bearings. But if we want to take a trip from Los Angeles to New York, we need more information, more detail.

By the same token, to understand exactly how the mind develops from birth to maturity, we must have more information than just the framework of the growing-up process. Framework, alas, does not give us the complete picture. For that we need to examine the integral *design* of the process that develops us psychologically.

~ 5 ~

Elements of Design

*J*ust as the blueprints of a house convey its most essential features, so the design of the process of psychological maturation conveys *its* most essential features. In this brief chapter I want to preview the design of this process. We shall undertake a more in-depth exploration of this subject in succeeding chapters.

The design of psychological maturation is like a living narrative. It is a story that tells us many things. It tells us:

- *How type-1 abilities are created.* We shall see what type-1 abilities do, how they function together within the mind, and how they form the system the mind will be using to interpret input from the outside world.
- *How type-1 abilities develop in a relatively fixed sequence.* Just as children crawl before they walk, and walk before they run, they develop certain psychological abilities before others. For example, a child is able to say yes before no, to feel shame before feeling guilt, to think concretely before thinking abstractly, and so on.[1]
- *How this unfolding sequence is unconsciously experienced as an*

inner path. Although a few individuals may experience aspects of the maturational path in some detail, most will probably experience it primarily as a desire to pursue a particular direction in life or a certain area of interest: to enter into or disengage from a relationship; to set aside time to develop job and career skills; to follow the road of self-development; or to spend extensive time alone. Because following the maturational path is essential to sustaining development over the course of immaturity, having some sense of this unconscious path is integral to one's growing-up process.

- *Why movement down this path is not automatic.* Each type-1 ability develops through a process that determines whether or not it will form correctly. Unfortunately, some will be compromised. An accumulation of compromised abilities can bring the entire maturational process to a halt, for they alter the mind's capacity to function effectively and devitalize the growing-up process. This is how some people become psychologically stuck, forever functioning in the stage of childhood, adolescence, or youth.

- *How the maturing person must engage in symbolic behavior for the mind to develop type-1 abilities,* and how symbolic behaviors may last for months or even years while the underlying abilities complete their development. This interplay between development and behavior will explain why rebelliousness, alienation, and the midlife crisis tend to last so long.

- *How the mind progressively expands its capacity to understand by repeating a simple formula.* The mind of early childhood can experience and understand only a limited portion of the world. It expands this understanding by gradually increasing the area of the world it can experience and then by developing the type-1 abilities it needs to deal with the newly expanded range. This *maturational formula—* increased range followed by development followed by greater range—is repeated many times over until the mind can experience and deal with the world at large.

- *How dramatic increases in range produce two of the three periods of normal crisis that occur during immaturity.* Most often increases in range occur in manageable portions, and the development required to deal with the new range soon follows. However, during the identity crisis and the midlife crisis, the increases are so extensive that it may take several years for the mind to develop the capacity to deal with the new range.

- *How the mind ultimately creates a fully correct understanding of the world.* At the end of the midlife crisis, type-1 ability formation ceases, the immature part of the life cycle comes to an end, and the person has reached maturity.

Finally, understanding the design of the process through which we become mature will tell us:

- How the mind thinks in immaturity and then in maturity
- Why some of us are "feelers" and some are "see-ers"
- How we use others in our lives to keep the mind stable, and what happens if these significant people should leave us
- Why dependency is an essential component of the growing-up process from birth through the midlife crisis
- Why people are afraid to die
- How the development of the mind influences the way we think about God

To begin to understand these and other issues, we will now start at the beginning—in very early childhood—and follow the first steps on the maturational path as a few scattered type-1 abilities gradually come together, eventually to form a fully functioning mind.

Part II

~~~

~ 6 ~

Establishing the Mind

*B*lind, hairless, barely able to pull itself along with its forelegs, and with its powerful hind legs not yet developed, the newborn kangaroo still somehow makes the seemingly impossible journey from the opening of the mother's birth canal to her warm, protective pouch. There it will spend the next several months attached to a life-giving nipple while continuing to develop physically. Only when its body parts and organ systems are fully differentiated will the young kangaroo be anatomically whole. And only then will it be physically capable of functioning outside the mother's pouch, joining the world in which it will live.

The human infant, by contrast, is born in a state of anatomical wholeness. Its body parts and organ systems have developed in sequence during gestation and are in place at birth. Only one major system—the mind—remains in a primitive, undifferentiated state.

The mind, much like an internal organ such as the heart or the liver, is best conceptualized as a distinct entity. Unlike the heart or liver, however, the mind cannot be physically isolated. It must be conceptually isolated just as, for example, physicists conceptually isolated the atom. And just as the models of physics draw the image of the atom as an isolated, singular entity—that of a spherical nucleus of protons and neutrons orbited by small, round electrons—so maturational theory will present the mind as an isolated, singular entity.

The story of psychological maturation is, first and foremost, the story of the gradual building of the mind in its increasing complexity. The process of its construction is an unconscious Herculean labor that will require almost continuous effort over some three decades. Only at the end of this time, and only with the successful resolution of the midlife crisis, will the mind be whole. Only then is a person capable of correctly understanding the world in which he or she lives. And only then is one capable of taking part in that world, fully equipped to begin the search for personal meaning and fulfillment.

How does the mind evolve from its earliest, undifferentiated state to fully formed maturity? Through what intermediate stages must it pass? How does it function along the path to maturity, and how does it function in the state of wholeness when maturity is achieved? Finally, what does possessing a mature mind enable us to do?

To answer these questions we must first look at the fundamental unit used in the mind's construction. This unit is the type-1 ability. It is to the construction of the mind what the atom is to the construction of matter, or the element to the composition of compounds. Type-1 abilities are the primary building blocks of the system the mind will use to understand the world. Yet just as molecules are not built out of any old kind or number of atoms, nor specific compounds constructed out of any chance combination of elements, the mind is more than an ever-building, random collection of psychological abilities. Rather, the mind is a product of the development of highly specific abilities assembled in highly specific ways.

Tracking the Mind

Over the span of psychological immaturity, thousands of individual type-1 abilities are created. Many are simple psychological actions that enable the mind to perform tasks patterned after physical movements. For example, the mind develops the ability to grasp and let go of; to reach, embrace, and hold on to; to move forward and stop; to draw lines.

Some type-1 abilities are patterned after what we see or hear. Examples include the ability to visualize thoughts as pictures or to hear thoughts as words, as well as to determine what will register during the thought process as foreground or background, as center or periphery, or as margins. Still other abilities are more purely conceptual—the ability to understand time and space or to say no or yes. But independent of their function, each of the thousands of type-1 abilities adds to and frames the progressive development of the mind.

Alone, each psychological ability is relatively unimpressive; but together, functioning as the mind, what they allow us to do is magically impressive. They allow us to experience, conceptualize, reason, understand, plan, act, solve problems. And together with type-2 abilities, they allow us to compose symphonies and write books; to explore mathematically the origin of the universe; to formulate the social, political, cultural, and religious frameworks by which we seek to organize our planet.

To accomplish these feats, the mind must grow from a loosely assembled collection of abilities into a well-working psychological system capable of transforming thousands of bits of information into a single understanding of the world. And while the mind is still incomplete and incapable of creating that fully correct understanding, it must be able to create some kind of coherent interim understanding. This seemingly unremarkable step—establishing a mind capable of creating a coherent, interim understanding of the world—is truly an accomplishment of monumental proportions. Once established, this capacity becomes the functional platform from which two and a half decades of continuous development will be launched.

The mind creates its interim understanding by using type-1 abilities to fulfill three of its basic maturational needs:

1. The need to reach and maintain a state of psychological stability, for only when the mind is stable can it remain oriented and focused
2. The need to secure the input it will ultimately shape into an understanding of the world
3. The need to be able to process this input and much more, to create a singular understanding of a given subject at any given time[1]

As we shall see in this chapter, the type-1 abilities that fulfill these three needs work in concert to determine *how* the mind goes about understanding the world. We shall also see how certain formations within the mind bear on that understanding.

Creating an Interim Understanding: The Mind's First Maturational Need— Securing Stability

TYPE-1 ABILITIES IN SUSPENDED EQUILIBRIUM

Type-1 abilities begin to develop in the earliest phases of the mother-infant relationship as small, discrete, free-floating psychological capacities. For these abilities to function together, there is a broader psychological requirement: They must be brought together into a stable form of *equilibrium*—a general requirement for all living things.

According to maturational theory, newly developing abilities are unconsciously experienced early in a child's life as being in general but loose proximity to one another. Like particles suspended in solution, these abilities simply exist, largely unconnected. The mind in this configuration is in the state of *suspended equilibrium.*

This mind is unstable, leading to an inconsistent interpretation of incoming data and a fluctuating understanding of the surrounding world. Both of these problems dissipate when the mind moves into a different form of equilibrium.

DYADIC EQUILIBRIUM

During the first few years of life, the child slowly develops the capacity to bring type-1 abilities into what is unconsciously experienced as closer proximity. This process of *consolidation* produces psychological stability.[2] Early in life, abilities consolidate primarily when the child engages in physical movement, such as walking or running. When movement stops, consolidation dissipates. Consolidation also takes place, but to a lesser degree, as the child listens to and looks at what goes on around him or her. Hearing the mother's voice, or playing with toys, causes the parts of the mind automatically to move closer together. But all these methods are rudimentary and relatively inefficient.

As time passes, this consolidation becomes more efficiently accomplished, and by two and a half years of age, a new and more effective method has evolved. Now it is looking at the mother's face that brings about consolidation within the child. When the mother leaves the room—or, from the child's point of view, disappears—the newfound consolidation is lost. When the mother returns and the child reestablishes visual contact with her, the mind again consolidates. The mother's face has functioned as the child's first *organizer*. In maturational theory, an organizer is any person, thing, activity, or idea that effects significant consolidation.

The capacity to consolidate through the use of organizers signals the beginning of a transformation into a new and higher form of psychological equilibrium. Because the mind needs an outside source of assistance (the organizer) to maintain this state of consolidation, I call it *dyadic equilibrium*—equilibrium consisting of two parts: the mind plus the organizer.

Within weeks, the child develops the capacity to use the *memory* of the mother's face as a temporary organizer. Now when she disappears, the child no longer needs to make visual contact with her to remain consolidated. Rather, he or she simply remembers her image. But memory fades. As the threat of deconsolidation sets in, the child seeks out the mother, sees her face again, and remains consolidated. Seeking out the mother's face to maintain consolidation is known as *checking-in behavior,* and only when this behavior is successful does the child feel free to go back to play.[3]

With movement into dyadic equilibrium, the mind has now developed the capacity to remain stable, because it can consistently consolidate through the use of the mother/organizer. From this point on, remaining stable becomes the child's most compelling psychological need. Furthermore, the need to consolidate through the use of organizers as a means of remaining stable continues throughout psychological immaturity.

Organizer → Consolidation → Stability

As the child continues to grow, his or her primary organizers evolve, remaining appropriate to the child's changing life experiences. For example, the mother's face expands to include the entire mother—enabling the child to check in from a distance. Within a year or two, she will be replaced as primary organizer by the father. In turn, mother and father will be replaced by friends, teachers, hobbies, schoolwork, and so on. In later life common organizers might include one's spouse, children, career, or possessions. Also, organizers tend to become multiple. For example, a woman's work, husband, and children may all have organizing qualities. There is also a tendency to move more toward self-organizing: an exercise regimen or self-development program may take on organizational qualities.

The organizers in one's life are easy to identify. They are those persons, things, activities, or ideas that are central and compelling. Regardless of their origin, organizers always perform the same function: They effect the consolidation of psychological abilities within the maturing mind, enabling it to remain stable.

The excessive use of one particular organizer can throw one's life temporarily out of balance. Consider the case of Chris, who at age thirty suddenly took up running. Within a short time, he increased his scheduled runs from three to seven days a week. Soon he began making plans for his first marathon. At social events he talked at length about his newly discovered sport. To accommodate and facilitate his daily runs, he changed his sleeping pattern, diet, and meal schedule, placing a strain on his relationship with his wife. Chris's apparent addiction to running reflects an excessive use of one organizer in an attempt to secure his psychological stability. Over several more months, Chris developed additional organizers, which allowed him to integrate his running into a more balanced psychological profile.

The process of consolidation also relies on many fail-safe systems. Children, for instance, carry with them pillows, blankets, pets, dolls, and other toys—transitional objects that can temporarily substitute for the organizing parent.[4] But maintaining stability by consolidating through the use of an organizer can be a risky matter. Sometimes we lose our organizers—parents die, school chums move away, couples divorce, children leave home, one may lose a job or retire.

The loss of an organizer always results in some deconsolidation, causing the mind to become unstable. In a state of instability, a person may feel a sense of "going to pieces," "coming apart," of being unable to "get oneself together," being "unable to function," or of simply being "deeply depressed." The result may be an aggressive move to secure and control the departing organizer or those remaining organizers vital to the mind's continued consolidation. During the time it takes to neutralize this threat, all other psychological tasks will be set aside. Indeed, the need for consolidation becomes as compelling as the need for water, air, or food. Only years later, with the successful resolution of the midlife crisis, will the mind evolve into a more sophisticated state, in which psychological stability is not dependent upon the use of outside organizers.

Consider how this dynamic plays itself out in the unhappy marriage of Mark and Lisa. Their twelve years together have been marked by a number of trial separations, but each break in the relationship has been brief, always ending in reconciliation. The fact is that Mark and Lisa's dilemma represents a common and predictable marital pattern—they can't live with each other, and they can't live without each other.

Lisa becomes immobilized by separation. The loss of her organizers—her husband and her marriage—is deconsolidating. She has difficulty collecting her thoughts and becomes overwhelmed by the prospect of independently providing for her future. Despair replaces her initial resolve to end the marriage; psychological instability translates into doubts about the wisdom of separating. Almost immediately she feels the ever-growing need to resume her relationship with Mark.

Mark's problem is even more acute. At work he is preoccupied with thoughts of Lisa; when he is alone, those thoughts are replaced by a sense of instability, a feeling that he is coming apart at the seams. Mark now tries to spend most of his time with other people, but even while he is with them he dreads the moment when he must be alone again. For Mark, the chronic unhappiness of his marriage is preferable—so it seems at the time—to the anxiety that accompanies separation.

What we have here are not just two people locked in an unsatisfying marriage but two people who function as each other's primary organizer. First coupled through marriage by church and state, they are now trapped by their mutual dependency. For each, separation is associated with the symptoms of deconsolidation.

In all probability, both Mark and Lisa had difficulty with the early development of the type-1 abilities that enable the mind to remain securely organized through a variety of organizers. Certainly both have ongoing problems now developing other organizers that would allow them to move on with their lives. Unable to correctly conceptualize and resolve their dilemma, Mark and Lisa remain stuck in a relationship that both of them need and neither truly wants.

The S_1 Carrier: The Functional Centerpiece of the Immature Mind

Just how does the organizer, something in the external world, effect consolidation and enable the mind to remain stable? Organizers ''work'' by stimulating the actions of an ''inner attractor,'' which I call an S_1 carrier (pronounced ''S one"). S_1 carriers are special type-1 abilities that function like powerful magnets deep in the mind; they seem to draw and hold individual abilities together and thereby effect consolidation. Here is a simple diagram of how they work:

Organizer → S_1 Carrier (magnet) → Consolidation (Dyadic Equilibrium) → Stability

Through the consistent use of the S_1 carrier, the child's mind by age three is firmly established in dyadic equilibrium—using outside organizers to effect consolidation. In so doing the mind has now achieved the capacity for a steady state of stability, fulfilling its first maturational need.

The S_1 carrier also plays a central role in fulfilling the mind's second need.

The Mind's Second Maturational Need: Securing Input

At birth, the infant has a highly limited capacity to experience the world psychologically, because sensory data that reach the brain do not continue through as input to the mind. Input to the mind is restricted to data that the mind gradually develops the ability to access. In other words, there is a naturally occurring protective barrier between what is physically recorded by the brain and what can be experienced by the mind. This barrier protects the child's mind from the hyperstimulation that would automatically result from unrestricted sensory input.

As the child matures, the mind must develop the ability actively to access information already available to the brain. This information provides the mind with most of the material it will use to conceptualize the world. The converse is also true: One's capacity to understand is limited by the information to which the mind has access.

Over the first five years of life, the mind slowly fills its need for input by developing those type-1 abilities that can access data conveyed to the brain through the body's five (perceptual) senses. The mind first utilizes taste and smell, but these senses play a limited role in understanding the world. Hearing and touch are integrated next, and the mind's capacity to access what can be seen is developed last.[5]

By age five or six, then, the child's mind should in theory have developed the capacity to access freely—in balance—all that can be experienced through the perceptual senses. In practice, however, the child rarely develops an uncompromised capacity to access all input; some compromise is generally the rule. But whether the ultimate configuration is correct or compromised, the balance is firmly established by age six and will remain unchanged throughout immaturity.

From this point on, people who are compromised in the capacity to access visually transmitted information will be overly dependent on hearing and touch to understand their world. Known as "feelers," they elevate emotions to a central position in life. Consequently, they will construct a somewhat simplistic and idealistic reality, in which such characteristics as trust, love, and caring play central, overvalued, and unrealistic roles. In the extreme, these people believe personal and universal problems can be solved completely by more loving, sharing, compassion, and so on.

Conversely, those whose minds are compromised in their capacity to access touch will be overly dependent on their capacity to see. Known as "see-ers," they tend to rely on the use of complex, visually based models to understand their world, while undervaluing the importance of the emotional dimensions of life. In the extreme, these people tend to be viewed as cold, heartless, and ruthless.[6]

The blend between seeing and feeling may differ from person to person. But whatever the balance, so long as the mind is using S_1 carriers to maintain stability, its understanding of the world will be created primarily from the perceptual senses. This means that even with an unrestricted and balanced capacity to access all input carried by the five senses, without the full use of the sixth sense, intuition, the maturing person's interim understanding of the world is based on incomplete information.

The Mind's Third Maturational Need: Processing Information

In addition to acting as magnets to effect consolidation and determining how the mind secures input (through the five senses), S_1 carriers play an important role in the way the mind processes information.

When we think, the thoughts we have are not free-floating. Rather, they are unconsciously experienced as attached or secured to an underlying S_1 carrier. The mind automatically perceives each thought as a "part" and proceeds to create a broader understanding of the subject by expanding the part into a "whole." For example, Person A, in making a judgment about Person B, may take one characteristic (or part) of Person B and then use this part to create the whole. So Janet may key on the fact that because Jim is tall, short, black, white, handsome, or ugly (all parts), he is completely good or bad (the whole). Or, in a broader context, the desire to limit the abuse of power (the part) can act as the basis for the concept of democracy (the whole). From any single thought (beginning/part), the immature mind—through the use of

S_1 carriers—creates an understanding that it experiences as the whole.[7]

Expanding the part into the whole can be remarkably serviceable. It permits a person—no matter how young, no matter how limited the perceptual input, no matter how impoverished the thought process—to believe that he or she is in command of a complete picture. This enables one to avoid feeling overwhelmed by the magnitude of the unknown and thus paralyzed by a sense of insufficiency.

Reviewing the Role of the S_1 Carrier in Creating an Interim Understanding of the World

By age four or five, the S_1 carrier has firmly established the child's mind in dyadic equilibrium. In so doing, it dictates *how* the mind under construction creates its interim understanding of the world. Here, the word *how* refers to the requirements imposed by the S_1 carrier that the mind will (1) use outside organizers to effect consolidation and stability; (2) access input through the five perceptual senses; and (3) think about the world by expanding the part to the whole. These three roles establish the S_1 carrier as the functional centerpiece of the immature mind. (See Figure 6.)

Maintaining Stability: Establishing and Then Retiring the S_1 Carrier

Were it not for the fact that the mind uses different types of S_1 carriers to think, this is all we would need to know about the role of carriers. However, five carriers develop over the first six years of life, each designed to transport a different kind of content. Failure to establish correctly each type of

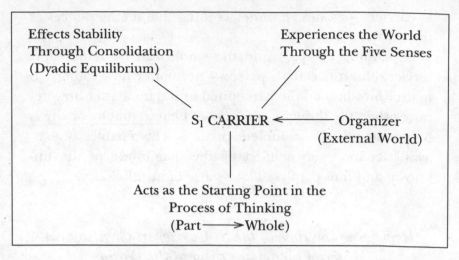

*The Role of the S_1 Carrier in the Mind's Creation of a
Stable Interim Understanding of the World*
FIGURE 6

carrier leaves the mind divided in purpose and somewhat unstable—a condition known as a *neurosis.*

In order of their development, the five S_1 carriers are:

- The *context carrier,* created in infancy and activated when
  the child is thinking about her or his surroundings
- The *maternal carrier,* used when the child is thinking about
  the mother
- The *self carrier,* emerging in early childhood and used
  when thinking about oneself
- The *father carrier,* which begins to develop at about age
  three or four and is used to think about the father
- The *model carrier,* the last to develop, used when thinking
  about everything not carried by the other carriers

Having access to these five carriers gives the child all that is
needed to think about an expanding world. But while the

child is thinking about whatever he or she needs to think about, the mind must also stay consolidated in order to remain stable in dyadic equilibrium. For this to happen, whatever the child thinks about must have a consolidating effect.

There are few problems with this system so long as the child spends most of the day at home. After all, much of a young child's thinking naturally includes the mother, one of the child's primary organizers, so remaining consolidated is usually not a problem. When three-year-old Eric, for example, uses the maternal carrier to think about his mother, this carrier automatically consolidates his mind in dyadic equilibrium. Thus Eric benefits from two functions of the maternal carrier—thinking and consolidating.

By age six, however, Eric will spend a good portion of his day away from home, in school. This could present a problem, because even though Eric's mind must still remain consolidated in order to remain stable, thinking about his mother is no longer a solution. At best, it distracts him from his schoolwork; at worst, it becomes preoccupying, even crippling. So how does Eric's mind remain consolidated?

By the time children enter school, they need to have outgrown their parents as (primary) organizers. In other words, by now Eric should have developed the ability to consolidate by thinking about things in an expanded world, not by having to think about his mother (or his father).

But how does a child outgrow the use of mother and father organizers? This task evolves out of a child's relationship with the parents. If the quality of Eric's relationship with his mother is sufficient, he develops the belief that she is a permanent part of his life. This sense of maternal permanence catalyzes a change within the maternal carrier, which results in Eric's no longer needing to think about his mother to effect consolidation. As a consequence of this important step, the child develops what I call *maternal constancy*. He or she can now use the maternal carrier simply to carry thoughts about the mother, not for the added purpose of effecting consolidation and maintaining stability.

Retiring the maternal carrier for consolidating paves the way for the use of the next carrier—the father carrier—for consolidating. As the child's attention shifts from mother to father, his or her compelling need to be with the mother ends. One phase of the mother-child relationship has now come to a close.

Again, effective fathering promotes *paternal constancy:* Once this occurs, the child no longer uses the father carrier to maintain consolidation. In turn, paternal constancy paves the way for the next carrier—the model carrier. Thus, both mother and father carriers have been outgrown as consolidating agents.

Establishing maternal and paternal constancy can be a confusing and emotionally wrenching experience for the young child. Moreover, the unconscious issues involved are clouded by other forms of type-1 ability development, particularly sexual. The resulting turbulence is what psychoanalysts call the Oedipal crisis.

By the time the child goes to school, only three of the five carriers should still have dual purposes (carrying thoughts and effecting consolidation)—the context carrier, the self carrier, and the model carrier. Because the context carrier is used when the child thinks about school; the model carrier when the child thinks about specific schoolwork, such as arithmetic; and the self carrier when the child thinks about him- or herself, it is easy for the child to think about schoolwork and still remain consolidated in dyadic equilibrium.

Figure 7 depicts the life span of each S_1 carrier as a consolidating agent.

Carrier					
Context	-- x				
Mother	--- x (mother constancy)				
Self	-- x				
Father	-------x (father constancy)				
Model	------------------------------- x				
Age	0	3	6	→	maturity

Life Span of S_1 Carriers as Consolidating Agents of Dyadic Equilibrium

FIGURE 7

Sometimes a child's mind may fail to develop maternal or paternal constancy. This was Jeff's dilemma. While he was in school, his mind naturally, and appropriately, used the model carrier to think about an arithmetic problem. But because Jeff had never achieved maternal constancy, he still had to use his maternal carrier to remain consolidated in dyadic equilibrium. As a result, Jeff had to switch back and forth in his use of carriers. In order to remain consolidated and stable when he was thinking about arithmetic with his model carrier, he would at some point also need to think about his mother with his maternal carrier. We now recognize this seeming inability to stay focused as a form of attention deficit disorder.[8] In a more severe case, a child like Jeff might develop a school phobia, feeling a compelling need to return home in order physically to "check in" with the mother and thereby remain consolidated.

Retiring the mother and father carriers as consolidators at the appropriate time is one of the mind's great accomplishments. It is what enables the older child to utilize a wide range of organizers in the external world to achieve psychological stability. This, in turn, is a critical component in maintaining a steady state of dyadic equilibrium—a fundamental requirement for creating a stable interim understanding of the world.

Psychological Structure and an Interim Understanding of the World

One of the more interesting aspects of maturational theory is the premise that some structures within the mind convey meaning and influence the way the immature mind creates its interim understanding of the world.[9] Such structures may be either isolated type-1 abilities or configurations composed of many individual abilities. The mind extracts meaning from these structures, and the meaning is perceived as knowledge. Such knowledge thus creates entire blocks of understanding about oneself and about the surrounding world. For instance, one's sense of self, one's understanding of responsibility, one's sense of inside and outside are all determined by structure within the mind. This knowledge supplements the understanding of the world we create through our formal thought process. Let us look at some examples, noting in each how structure creates knowledge.

A SENSE OF SELF

At about age two and a half, the child's mind takes a quantum leap forward when it develops the capacity to consolidate individual psychological abilities enough to experience an unconscious sense of inner form. It is somewhat like consolidating water molecules enough to create a cloud in the sky. A sense of inner form is what enables the child to experience a sense of self:

Consolidation → Inner Form → Sense of Self

To clarify this principle further, consider the following metaphor: A chair consists of individual particles, or atoms. If we could move these atoms out of the chair, the chair as we know it would fall apart and ultimately vanish. But the essential particles of the chair—the atoms—would still be present in the room. If we could then reconsolidate the atoms, the form of the chair would reappear. This is analogous to creating form within the mind through consolidation—form experienced as a sense of self.

Note that the child is not born with this self-awareness, nor is it learned. Rather, a sense of self automatically accompanies the experience of inner form that results from early stages of consolidation in dyadic equilibrium.

INSIDE FROM OUTSIDE

With a sense of self in place, the mind has a basis for distinguishing inside from outside. This is because the mind can use the sense of self as an inner point of reference, enabling the person to know that his or her thoughts are coming from within and are therefore "mine." Distinguishing one's thoughts as "mine" acts to stabilize a sense of self and a sense of "other." When we interact, for example, I know that your thoughts are coming from you and my thoughts are coming from me. People with similar thoughts now feel they have something in common. Widely accepted ideas are known as *consensual reality*.

Without the reference point provided by a sense of self, thoughts could be attributed to anything—outside or inside—that can be seen, felt, or otherwise experienced. Indeed, on rare occasions, when a sense of self is lost, one's thoughts may be misconstrued as originating from the outside—a phenomenon known as hallucinating. In this case, reality is constructed not on shared but on highly personalized input, and a stable, consensual reality becomes impossible to achieve. Again, this sense of inside/outside arises out of the structure of dyadic equilibrium. It is not learned, nor is it developed as the direct result of a specific type-1 ability.

A SENSE OF BEING A PERSON

After the child establishes a sense of self, further consolidation creates an *advanced* sense of inner form. This gives rise to a sense that "I am a person":

Early Consolidation → Early Sense of Inner Form → Sense of Self → Further Consolidation → Advanced Sense of Inner Form → "I am a person"

Normally, the mind in dyadic equilibrium remains in a state of advanced consolidation, and the knowledge that "I am a person" can be taken for granted. But under extreme circumstances, deconsolidation can proceed to the point where one's sense of being a person is threatened. It can occur, for example, with the abrupt loss of an organizer. Also, as we shall see, it happens as a matter of course during the midlife crisis. The result is a feeling of impending death, the fear that "I am about to die." This unconscious equation between the loss of being a person and the threat of death triggers powerful resistance to further deconsolidation. The threat must be rendered harmless immediately. The usual result is an aggressive move toward reconsolidation, most often through controlling and thereby stabilizing one's organizers.

The S_1 Carrier as Structure

There are many other instances in which components of the mind manifest themselves as specific knowledge about the world. As one of those components, the S_1 carrier plays a major role in determining what we feel, think, and believe about the world we live in.[10]

THE CONCEPT OF INDIVIDUAL RESPONSIBILITY

A person's concept of responsibility helps shape, over time, the role he or she plays in society. Those who experience themselves as responsible for their own lives see education and personal development as critical to success; they actively work to secure their place in the world. Those who believe that responsibility originates on the outside see themselves as "entitled"; they tend to fall back on the work of others to provide them with a life.

According to maturational theory, one's concept of responsibility is automatically determined by the unconsciously perceived placement of carriers within the mind. If the child's carriers are unconsciously experienced as being on the inside, then the child views him or herself as responsible for his or her own life. Children who experience their carriers as being outside view others as responsible for their lives.

The quality and consistency of care a child receives during the first two years of life are the determining factors in the development of the concept of responsibility. If the relationship with the mother is experienced as "safe," the child develops the capacity to experience its carriers as internal. But if for some reason the relationship is experienced as potentially "unsafe," the carriers will be experienced as being on the outside. Once established, this configuration will almost certainly persist throughout life.

Unconsciously experiencing carriers as external is a subtle compromise within the mind. Although it causes little personal conflict, it may well be the most common flaw in the mind's construction. In fact, a compelling argument can be made that entire social systems, forms of government, and philosophies of law and order arise from this misconstruction. Be that as it may, the belief that someone or something else—whether another person, society, or government— is responsible for one's life is an inappropriate position, developmentally speaking. It is caused by compromise in the basic integrity of the mind. The position "I am fundamentally responsible for my own life" reflects correct development.

THE S_1 CARRIER AND A SENSE OF HAVING A MIND

Having a mind and experiencing one's mind are two different phenomena. The actual mind is ever-present, converting psychological data into an understanding of the world. But having a sense of one's mind (or the sense of having a mind)—with thoughts roaming around inside one's head— is still another artifact of dyadic equilibrium. In fact, a person who loses the capacity to maintain dyadic equilibrium not only feels out of control as a result of deconsolidation but also has the attendant feeling of "losing my mind." (And those who mature beyond the limits of dyadic equilibrium experience themselves as having outgrown or given up their immature minds.) So the experience of having a mind changes with fluctuations in dyadic equilibrium and with the passage of time, even though the actual presence of the mind remains constant.

BEYOND CARRIERS

Within the background created by the greater space of the mind, carriers are unconsciously experienced as single foci—somewhat like stars in the broad reaches of the sky. This spatial background has its own unique psychological reality. For what exists beyond all carriers (beyond all form) is unconsciously experienced by the mind as God. This means that one's psychological experience of God is, at least in part, tied to the structure of the mind—just as other forms of knowledge are.

While God is unconsciously experienced as being beyond all form, one's thoughts about God are attached to the last developed carrier. This means that the mind automatically assigns to God the *characteristics* of this last carrier. As a result, those who are using primarily early context carriers to carry thoughts tend to experience God as part of the everyday environment. In this situation the sun, moon, fire, and/or water may be seen as divine. Those who use primarily mother carriers to carry thoughts experience God as maternal. Those who use primarily father carriers experience God as "God the Father." Those who use primarily model carriers will experience God in the form of a model—a God of love, compassion, wisdom, and so on. Throughout immaturity, one's concept of God evolves to correspond with evolving structure within the mind. Only with the accomplishment of psychological maturity will the built-in reality of God become constant.

That the experience of God is built into our psychological structure (and our psychological structure evolves over the course of immaturity) is one reason why—usually throughout life—everyone struggles on some level with the issue of a divine being. But why should this experience be built in? Why do we not experience this spatial background simply as a void? The answer remains a mystery, but the result compels each of us—through the inherent design of the mind, if you will—first to be aware of God as an idea and then to struggle over time with questions about the nature of God's existence.

Putting It All Together

Let us step back for a moment and review the steps by which, according to maturational theory, the mind establishes itself. As I have shown, the mind evolves within a few short years from an unstable collection of type-1 abilities in suspended equilibrium to a stable and highly complex instrument in dyadic equilibrium—from an unstable entity totally dependent on the presence of the parents to a stable configuration capable of functioning independently.

By age six, the child's mind has constructed within itself a system of abilities capable of creating an interim understanding of the world. The most important component of this system is the S_1 carrier, a type-1 ability located deep within the unconscious. Its use determines how the mind under construction functions. The use of the S_1 carrier dictates that the mind: (1) will be dependent on external organizers to effect consolidation and psychological stability; (2) will process input primarily from the first five senses to create its understanding of the world; and (3) will create during the thought process a sense of sufficient understanding by expanding the part to the whole.

While an interim understanding of the world is immensely functional, it is achieved through significant compromise. It is created out of incomplete information (only five senses); by the use of something in the external world (outside organizers to create psychological stability); and with only the illusion of completeness (by expanding the part to the whole).

This interim understanding is then supplemented by knowledge arising from the structure of the mind. Of particular importance is the sense of self—an awareness created through enough consolidation to provide a sense of form within the mind. A sense of self establishes a point of reference, which the mind then uses to localize thoughts. This, in turn, becomes an important component of the mind's capacity to distinguish inside from outside. Specifically, it enables the child to create an understanding of the world that can be accepted by groups of others—an experience commonly known as consensual reality.

This psychological framework, firmly established by mid-childhood, remains essentially intact through the balance of immaturity. As we shall see, over the next two and a half decades the mind—while remaining in dyadic equilibrium— will systematically expand its capacity to understand the world.

~ 7 ~

The Maturational Process: How It "Works"

To understand the inner mechanisms of psychological maturation, we need to focus on that component of the mind which is the driving force behind its progressive construction. I call this component the *maturational process.* It is responsible for:

- Expanding the mind's range of understanding;
- Ultimately establishing and assembling enough type-1 abilities to produce a mature mind;
- Facilitating movement along the maturational path through tension reduction; and
- Promoting adherence to the path.

In this chapter, we shall look closely at this remarkable process. We shall also look at how other influences—schooling, parenting, self-development—affect a person's trek toward maturity. And we shall spend some time on what I believe is one of the most fascinating manifestations of the maturational process—symbolic engagement in the world.

The Maturational Process:
Function 1: Expanding the Mind's Range of
Understanding

The maturational process moves the mind toward maturity primarily by creating and assimilating new type-1 abilities. These, as we noted earlier, form out of an unconscious path. At birth, the infant has already traversed an analogous path, which gave rise to the growth and development of the body. The maturational path holds the potential to establish a complementary psychological whole. But components of the mind must develop through an additional three decades until—if all goes well—the mind becomes fully mature.

The maturational process promotes movement along this path through a series of usually small, repetitive steps. The first of these enables the mind to experience a manageable portion of the environment. This portion, or *range,* is what one unconsciously experiences as "psychologically real"—a term designed to distinguish it from a world created solely through learning. For example, by the time they are six, children have learned that countries exist in other parts of the world. But because of their limited range, the only world psychologically real to them is that of home, neighborhood, and other frequently visited areas.

As time passes, the mind's range is extended. Once a new range is established, enough type-1 abilities will be created to enable one effectively to understand and function within it. When this state is reached, the mind's range is once again extended. And so on.

The newborn's world is limited to its most immediate environment. Accordingly, earliest development is restricted primarily to creating type-1 abilities that enable the infant to function within this minuscule range: psychologically focusing, grasping, holding on to and letting go of, and recognizing primitive tonal and visual-spatial patterns. In time the constricted world of infancy expands to include home and family, then neighborhood and friends, school and schoolwork, the extended community, and so on. Again, with each extension of range, specific type-1 abilities must be developed to enable the maturing person to deal with this new world.

This simple formula—an expanded range followed by development within the range—repeats itself hundreds of times. Ultimately the mind's range includes the world at large, and the progressively constructed mind then positions the person to create a fully correct understanding of that world.

This pattern is depicted in Figure 8.

The Maturational Process:
Function 2: Establishing the Type-1 Ability—
A Five-Step Sequence

Throughout the maturational process, each type-1 ability will be created through a five-step sequence. In this sequence, the developing person unconsciously: (1) experiences a new ability as a need; (2) seeks out a special person called an *actualizer*, who "understands"; (3) practices the ability; (4) receives "permission" to develop—and thereby actualize—the ability; and (5) integrates the ability into the functioning mind. Let us look at what happens in each of these steps.

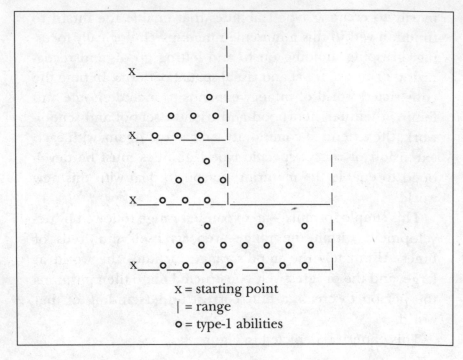

Relationship Between Range and Development of
Type-1 Abilities
FIGURE 8

1. EXPERIENCING A NEW ABILITY AS A NEED

The child first experiences a newly developing psychological ability as a need that may take a variety of forms. For example, the psychological ability to hold on to—in its early stages—may be experienced as a literal need to hold on to a blanket. Or it may be experienced figuratively as needing to hold obstinately on to a position. The psychological ability to draw a line may take the form of actually drawing a line with a crayon, or figuratively drawing a line by not letting a little brother into the room. Independent of the form taken, a newly developing type-1 ability is always unconsciously experienced as a need.

2. SEEKING AN ACTUALIZER

Upon experiencing a psychological need, the child seeks out someone he or she intuitively believes "understands" that need. For the very small child, that person usually is the mother, and the task of seeking is merely a matter of waiting for her to show up. Later on a parent, grandparent, or special friend may fulfill this requirement. Still later teachers, coaches, clergy, spouses, therapists, role models, mentors, and so on are invested with this role. I call these people *actualizers,* for it becomes their role to help actualize, or "make good," the development of the newly emerging type-1 ability.

3. PRACTICING THE ABILITY

The emerging ability is then practiced in the presence of the actualizer. *Practicing behavior* means that the developing person repeatedly acts in a way that demonstrates the ability in formation. For example, practicing the ability that will enable the child psychologically to grasp compels the child to grasp physically. This may take the form, say, of repeatedly grasping a toy. Or the newly emerging ability psychologically to let go of may be consciously experienced as a need repeatedly to let go of—to throw or drop—that same toy. The child now practices the behavior for as long as it takes him or her to understand how to do it.

4. ACTUALIZING THE ABILITY

The fourth and perhaps most crucial step in the process is catalyzed by the actualizer. His or her response to the practicing behavior triggers the final construction of the newly emerging ability. This interchange is known as *actualization*. To the child, this process is unconsciously perceived as permission, which must be granted and received before the emerging ability is firmly established in its final form and development can move forward.

Optimally, each new type-1 ability develops in pure form. By this I mean that one develops an unconditional capacity to perform that ability. For example, the eighteen-month-old develops the unbridled, pure capacity to say no. The child's secondary task is to determine when and how best to use this new ability. This principle remains in force throughout immaturity.[1]

The most common problem in ability formation is caused by a repeatedly conditional response from the actualizer. His or her conditions or qualifications often become built into the structure of the newly developing ability. When this happens, the ability becomes—and may remain—compromised.

As an example, let us revisit our eighteen-month-old who has begun to say no. Saying no is, one hopes, an acceptable part of the growing-up process. One also hopes that the child will be allowed not only the time to develop the pure ability but also the time to begin to determine when and how to use it properly.

But a child may sense from the responses of the actualizer that saying no is bad, or that it is risky to say no to someone in authority. From this point on, this person will feel bad each time he or she says no or will feel too intimidated to say no to someone in authority. All too frequently the unfortunate solution to this situation is to try to become everything to everybody in order to avoid the troublesome feelings that accompany saying no. (Adults with this problem often report the sense of never having truly been able to say no.)

Actualizers are crucial to development, for their responses determine, to some degree, whether type-1 abilities are correctly formed. Through their participation in the life of a developing person, these people create characteristics that are carried forward in the structure of the mind. So important is their contribution that the most significant actualizers in one's life may be consciously recognized as people of whom one might say, "I owe my chance in life" or "I owe who I am" to them.

Conversely, some actualizers respond to newly emerging abilities in ways that consistently compromise—or even block—their correct development. I call such people *pseudoactualizers*. If psychological development is to proceed normally, it must do so in spite of their influence.

5. INTEGRATING THE ABILITY

The five-step sequence is complete when the newly developed ability is finally integrated into the mind's overall functioning. This happens as a natural consequence of development and requires no elaboration.

Figure 9 depicts the entire five-step sequence of the development of a type-1 psychological ability.

Unconsciously experiencing a newly emerging ability as a need →

  Seeking an actualizer who understands →

    Practicing behavior →

     Actualizing the ability →

      Integrating it into the functioning of the mind

The Five-Step Sequence of Developing a Type-1 Ability
FIGURE 9

A final comment: As maturation proceeds, one progressively develops the capacity to perform for oneself each step of the five-step sequence. Through type-1 ability development, one comes to understand best one's own needs and can develop the capacity to grant oneself permission. When this step is taken, permission from others becomes developmentally meaningless. The combination of self-understanding and self-permission enables the maturing person to become self-actualizing—to be able to develop correctly independent of outside responses.[2] The development of a capacity for self-actualization is accompanied by a sense of freedom that truly reflects a newfound relationship with the world.

The Maturational Process:
Function 3: Reducing Tension

Let us return for a moment to the formula of expanding range followed by development, in which each increase in range automatically, if only temporarily, creates a developmental deficiency. This leads to a unique problem: The mind experiences this deficiency as an internal void. In immaturity a void is always associated with some degree of tension. Such tension may span a continuum from simple anxiety to a sense of being stretched and, if unchecked, to being overwhelmed or panicked.

The permanent corrective to this problem is the development of type-1 abilities that enable the mind to deal effectively with the increase in range. But new development takes time. Meanwhile, the tension associated with the void must be lowered to acceptable limits (psychologists call it a state of *optimal tension*) if development is to proceed smoothly.

The maturational process can lower the tension experienced by the mind in one or more of three ways. It can *borrow;* it can *negate* part of the increase in range; and/or it can *rework* already established but compromised type-1 abilities.

BORROWING

In *borrowing,* the maturational process moves to fill the internal void by treating an external person or thing as if it were part of the mind. Once borrowed, it fills the void, thereby decreasing the deficit. As a result, the tension disappears. Usually the mind borrows a person or (more correctly) that part of a person the mind unconsciously experiences as possessing the yet-to-be-developed abilities. The concept of borrowing is the basis for the old adage "It takes two to make one."

Consider Jason, a young child who wants to play outdoors but feels uncomfortable in that still-strange environment. Jason's psychological range has been extended to the outdoors, but he has not yet developed the abilities that would enable him to deal effectively with being outside. He experiences the deficit as a void, and this discomfort makes him reluctant to play outside. But when Jason is accompanied by Scott, a friend he believes "knows how to play outdoors," his mind "borrows" the imagined abilities of this friend, and his sense of discomfort dissipates.

An example of how this process might function later in life is illustrated in the case of Allison, a high school graduate who decided to attend a college far from home. Allison's mother brought her to my office because as the time grew near for her to leave, she became increasingly frightened. She couldn't sleep and was beginning to fear she had made a terrible mistake in her choice of college. As it turned out, this young woman did not need to see a psychiatrist after all. She soon learned that a friend was going to the same school, and her symptoms quickly disappeared. Naturally, she was happy just to have the companionship of a friend, but at a deeper level, the borrowing process enabled her psychologically to feel that the two of them together could face the unknown.

Borrowing can also involve possessions or experiences. For example, money, a home, a new car, even going to a certain school or knowing an admired person can fill an internal void. Normally, borrowing is a temporary solution. It works until the mind develops missing type-1 abilities. Unfortunately, one downside of borrowing is that it often results in an unconscious (and sometimes conscious) sense of possessiveness and dependency.[3] And if whoever is being borrowed from—such as a girlfriend or boyfriend—threatens to leave, there emerges a need to control the person in order to preserve what is being borrowed. Indeed, possessiveness, dependency, and the need to control almost always indicate an active borrowing process. As the need to borrow decreases, there is a corresponding decrease in dependency, and the compulsion to monitor and control also disappears. Failing to understand this interrelationship results in misconceptualizing the dynamics of dependency, possessiveness, and control—thus adding to the burden of developing the mind correctly.

NEGATION

Another mechanism designed to decrease psychological tension is *negation*. Simply put, the mind treats an established part of itself as if it does not exist. This narrows the range within which the mind must operate and thereby lowers tension.

A common form of negation is *compartmentalization*, in which a substantial range is treated as if it were made up of separate compartments or rooms. The mind then treats only selected areas as psychologically real at any given time. This eases the tension that would be caused by experiencing the whole.

For example, Dan finds himself overwhelmed by the demands of career and family. As an unconscious solution, he begins to treat his career as a compartment separate from his home life. He directs virtually all his attention to his work at the risk of temporarily neglecting his wife and children. Negation reduces the range Dan has to deal with, and he is then able fully to meet the developmental demands of a single compartment instead of being overwhelmed by the greater demands of the whole.

Negation is extremely useful for dealing with tension. Almost everyone uses it at some point. But, like borrowing, negation is only a temporary solution. Problems invariably arise when important factors are negated and then continuously ignored.

REWORKING

In everyone's life, many type-1 abilities are compromised during development. Like correctly formed abilities, they are integrated into the mind. But because they cannot fully perform their intended tasks, they create tension and may leave us with the feeling that something is not quite right. *Reworking* is the process of making right or completing development that was compromised earlier in life.

Reworking is commonplace—a relatively silent but indispensable part of the growing-up process. As a rule, the more isolated and recent the compromised development, the easier it is to rework. More difficult is the attempt to rework the products of early development—compromised abilities now being expressed in the form of bothersome symptoms.

In this case, therapeutic intervention may be required. In fact, the reworking of compromised abilities is the basis for most current forms of in-depth psychotherapy.

All three options—borrowing, negation, and reworking—are effective in lessening the tension caused by normal developmental deficits. All are crucial to a well-functioning maturational process. However, each is but a means to an end, and the end is always the development of those new type-1 abilities that enable the mind to deal with an expanded range.

Sometimes borrowing, or negation, or even reworking can become an end in itself. When this occurs, the tension-reducing process takes on an aura of permanence. Borrowing becomes a hopeless state of dependency. Negation results in permanently skewed interests. And reworking leads to a therapeutic orientation in which self-development becomes a never-ending quest to correct one's deficiencies. Each pattern leads to *maturational arrest* through the same predictable sequence. A person first feels a sense of stagnation. Over time stagnation gives way to a sense of "being stuck," and, unless corrected, being stuck leads to maturational arrest. At that point, there is a minimum of new type-1 ability formation, and the mind is left permanently to function in an incomplete state.

The Maturational Process:
Function 4: Adherence to the Path

The fourth task of the maturational process is to promote adherence to the unfolding maturational path. We are all inherently capable of reaching psychological maturity, but actually reaching that goal is in no way guaranteed.

One deterrent is making permanent commitments—to

marriage, parenthood, a career, and so on—before we are psychologically ready. Yet in our society early youth marks the appropriate time to make these commitments. In fact, our prevailing beliefs hold that doing so opens the way to true maturity and happiness. It is expected that sometime in one's twenties one should marry, have children, and get on with a permanent job or career. But maturational theory holds that commitments made in youth can easily turn out to be premature and detrimental to ongoing psychological maturation. The demands of such commitments may actually compete with those of the maturational process. This competition frequently forces the maturational path to be partially or completely abandoned.

The maturational process hedges against such abandonment in two ways. First, the process of developing to maturity is preemptive. The developing person is unconsciously compelled to satisfy the needs associated with newly emerging type-1 abilities rather than to meet the requirements of other commitments. In practice this means the primary interests of a maturing person are usually concentrated in areas that promote type-1 development. For instance, a heightened interest in politics may be a way of promoting the underlying development of abilities needed to understand the extended environment. Or certain relationships may unconsciously be chosen because of the presence of qualities suitable for borrowing.

Second, augmenting the preemptive effect of the process of psychological maturation is an "internal guidance system" of positive and negative feelings. Maturation that is working produces positive feelings—love, happiness, appreciation, and joy—that act as rewards for past progress and as incentives for continued development. Negative feelings, in reasonable doses, also promote continued development. Because they stem from compromised abilities, these abilities must be reworked to resolve the negative feelings. And re-working abilities, we now know, promotes movement along the maturational path.

Negative feelings can include shame, which may stem from early compromise in the type-1 abilities that create one's body image; humiliation, which reflects early compro-mised development in the capacity to function socially in the world; jealousy, which indicates difficulty in experiencing in-dependent action, the concept that the actions of others do not include the person; and guilt, which is experienced when one fails to live up to one's own models.

If the compromised abilities causing the negative feelings are not reworked, the feelings can easily become excessive and lead to nonproductive or even destructive behavior. For example, shame and humiliation can result in immobility, withdrawal, or retreat. Jealousy can lead to rage, thereby obscuring the need to develop correctly the capacity to con-ceptualize independent action. Excessive guilt leads to avoid-ance or to inappropriately changing behavior rather than appropriately changing models.

One additional feeling deserves special mention: that of being "snuffed out." It comes from a sense of impending maturational arrest—the cessation of movement down the maturational path. And when some outside factor is felt to be causing this feeling, the implications can be overwhelming. For whatever is viewed as competing with ongoing develop-ment—one's job, profession, even one's marriage and fam-ily—may be abandoned to preserve the freedom to mature.

Finally, no discussion of adherence to the maturational path would be complete without mentioning personal in-stinct. Many people are on some level in touch with their own maturational process; they have an almost uncanny sense of what "works" developmentally. Given a chance, these individuals gravitate naturally toward maturationally correct solutions, even when such solutions may be at odds with the prevailing wisdom and the wishes of those around them. Some, for example, may experience a driving need to be alone for extended periods of time—free from the demands of intense relationships. Others may find themselves wanting to pursue a particular experience that, although completely "out of character," seems crucial at the time. All such behaviors have as a likely common denominator the drive to facilitate the maturational process.

Putting It Together

The four primary tasks of the maturational process—establishing range, developing type-1 abilities, alleviating tension, and promoting adherence to the maturational path—seem clear and straightforward when spelled out in sequence on the printed page. But in the living, growing mind, more than one of these tasks may well be unconsciously operating at the same time.

For example, the maturing person may need to practice one developing—but not yet actualized—ability while seeking an actualizer for another newly developing ability. At the same time, he or she may be actively borrowing from still another source, while negating those feelings that, if fully experienced, might be overwhelming. And all this must be attended to while dealing with the wishes of others and the complex demands of daily life.

Such a multifaceted process cannot possibly be consciously regulated. Instead, regulation occurs through a steering mechanism within the maturational process, which determines when and how best to respond to the ever-changing requirements of the developing mind.[4] Following a path that conforms to these requirements creates a nonspecific pattern when it comes to living one's life. This pattern is known as a *random walk*. Only the freedom to pursue a random walk for the first three decades of life—and possibly beyond—offers the opportunity to nurture fully the ongoing needs of the maturational process.[5] For the developing person, then, this freedom is essential to becoming psychologically mature.

The Maturational Process and Symbolic Engagement

In essence, the formula for psychological maturation—range expansion, followed by ability development, followed by range expansion—is explicit, unambiguous. At heart it is a process of biting off, as it were, a manageable chunk of the world and then developing the capacity to digest it. With each cycle the mind increases some facet of its capacity to understand. To complete the picture, we add the two other components of the maturational process that function in tandem with the formula: the regulation of tension via borrowing, negation, and reworking; and adherence to the maturational path through the use of positive and negative feelings.

What we now have is a portrait of the unconscious process of psychological maturation as it might be seen from the perspective of the mind's eye. But only a tiny portion of this process can be observed in everyday behavior. And even then it appears somewhat "disguised."

In daily life, practicing and actualizing behaviors may show themselves as elements in our work and play, in our friendships, and even in our intimate relationships. Borrowing is apt to be expressed as a particular type of relationship and occasionally as possessiveness, dependency, and control. Negation may be acted out as patterns of avoidance or omission. And reworking can take the form of "coming to terms" with one's mother, father, childhood, and so on. Pressure to adhere to the path may be expressed through feelings such as love and joy, or humiliation and guilt.

I use the term *symbolic engagement* to refer to all expressions of the maturational process that characterize type-1 ability development, which, though open to simple observation, must be decoded for the underlying meaning to be understood.

Symbolic engagement has two components. *Symbolic behavior* is the *action* component: for example, the oppositional behavior of refusing to eat peas and carrots. *Symbolic reality* is what is *consciously* experienced: "I don't like and won't eat peas and carrots!" Adam, for example, has no awareness that his dislike of peas and carrots is in any way linked to the development of his mind. Nor does Chris—the runner training for his first marathon—realize that his behavior is symbolic and, as such, is linked to the development of his mind.

Almost any behavior during immaturity is likely to be symbolic, from the various facets of relationship formation to most forms of work and play. Symbolic reality can include opinions and beliefs about everything from peas and carrots to one's positions on social and political policy.

Symbolic engagement is, for me, one of the most fascinating aspects of the growing-up process. It functions as the interface between, on the one hand, an unconscious maturational process that depends on symbolic engagement to complete the mind under construction and, on the other hand, a society that, in the absence of decoding, misconstrues its entire nature and purpose.

The Profile of Symbolic Engagement

For almost a century, behavioral scientists have known that understanding the development that takes place during the first two decades of life facilitates psychological maturation. I hope it will become increasingly clear that this concept applies also to development taking place in the third and fourth (and beyond) decades of life. Here, too, decoding symbolic engagement enables one to frame specific maturational issues in a way that will enhance one's chances of correctly developing new type-1 abilities, thereby promoting further movement along the maturational path.

But to decode symbolic behavior, behavioral scientists must first recognize it. Fortunately, there are four characteristics that indicate that behavior is most probably symbolic:

- Symbolic behavior is central and compelling in one's life, often appearing to be virtually a matter of life or death. From the perspective of the developing person, each next step seems the most important. Failure to secure a series of steps raises the specter of the mind under construction being "snuffed out." This, in turn, creates a sense of urgency, which is often expressed as driven behavior. A good example is the behavior of the young antiwar protesters during the Vietnam War. Their opposition to the war knew no barriers. No obstacle was seen as insurmountable, no opponent too formidable, and no venue for expression could intimidate them.
- Symbolic behavior is not amenable to change through discussion. No amount of reasoning or cajoling can convince a young child that peas and carrots really taste good. After all, taste is scarcely the issue.
- Some forms of symbolic behavior are limited to a particu-

lar stage of life. For example, rebelliousness should occur in adolescence, alienation in youth.

- Symbolic behavior is phasic. Once the underlying type-1 abilities are developed, the particular form of symbolic behavior stops. It will be replaced by the symbolic behavior appropriate to the next set of developing abilities. When a bride says, six months or a year after her wedding, "What did I ever see in him, anyway?" or when an inveterate shopper asks, "Why did I buy all those clothes I didn't need and never wear?" or when a former sailing enthusiast wonders, "Why did I ever buy that sailboat in the first place?" the answer is: These people were all acting symbolically. When the underlying type-1 abilities formed, the connected behaviors were no longer maturationally relevant. As a consequence, their interests waned, and these phases gave way to the next. This phenomenon sheds light on how it is that most of the young activists of the Vietnam era eventually came to resolve their internal sense of alienation and today contribute to society as mainstream Americans. Yet these same men and women currently struggle with their midlife crises—symbolic behaviors now appropriate to their more advanced position on the maturational path.

Symbolic engagement is the arena in which the struggle to construct the mind is played out. It is here, over a span of three decades, that the fate of the mind under construction will be determined. But in everyday life, this expression of the maturational process is fraught with enormous problems. At best it is a haphazard and inefficient method of constructing something so vital as the human mind. Nonetheless, it is the mechanism our species is stuck with. The task for each of us is to understand its true meaning, for only then can we consciously nurture the process.

~ 8 ~

Architecture of the Mind

At this point, one can choose between two levels to continue to describe how the mind develops the system it uses to understand the world. The broader level would explore the system as a whole, from the perspective of its overall design. This approach would focus on the system's larger parts: different groups of abilities and how they function, as well as the patterns they form within the system. The other level, the more fundamental, is that of the individual type-1 ability. Here, the discussion would center on the development of each ability. For our purposes, however, it is probably best to stay away from this level. Although it might be possible to talk about the mind in terms of the development of each type-1 ability, it would surely be a time-consuming chore. Because there are thousands, perhaps tens of thousands of abilities— most with multiple functions—as a practical matter this type of modeling would be twenty-first-century psychology. Anyone wishing to model the process of psychological maturation at this level should bring a Cray computer and a hearty lunch.

It would be easier to talk about the process from the perspective of the other level: the larger parts of the system, and the system as a whole. This approach reduces the enormously complicated process of how the mind constructs its capacity to understand to a far more accessible sequence of concepts.

To do this, we must begin by looking at how the mind fulfills some of its basic maturational needs. The groups of abilities that fulfill these needs are the parts that will allow us to see how the system functions as a whole.

The Mind's Basic Maturational Needs

Maturational theory isolates six needs integral to the construction of the mind, three of which were discussed in Chapter 6. The six needs are to:

1. Create stability
2. Experience all input
3. Process information
4. Develop new psychological abilities
5. Create concepts
6. Form relationships

The abilities that fulfill these needs can be arranged into groups:

- *Group A abilities* are those that fulfill the mind's first three maturational needs: to create stability, experience all input, and process information. These abilities determine *how* the mind goes about creating its understanding of the world. During immaturity the word *how* refers to the fact that the mind (1) creates a stable, interim understanding; (2) uses input primarily from the five senses; and (3) understands a subject by starting with some part of the subject.

- *Group B abilities* satisfy only the mind's need to develop new abilities. In effect Group B abilities simply expand the ability pool in the other groups. Because these abilities play only a supportive role in the construction of the mind, they need no longer concern us.
- *Group C abilities* fulfill the mind's needs to create concepts and form relationships. They play a central role in the formula the mind uses to expand its range. Group C abilities thus determine not *how* the mind understands the world, but *how much* of the world it understands.

Sorted into groups, the abilities that fulfill the mind's six maturational needs look like this:

Abilities that

Create stability	Group A . . . Determines *how* the
Experience all input	mind goes about
Process information	understanding
Develop new abilities	Group B
Create concepts	Group C . . . Determines *how much*
Form relationships	the mind can understand

Patterns in the Maturational Process

Throughout immaturity, the abilities that develop to fulfill the mind's maturational needs form a distinct pattern of distribution. One might say this pattern offers a bird's-eye view of psychological maturation. We can learn from this pattern not only when most psychological development occurs but also such information as why there are three crisis periods during immaturity and why they crop up when they do.

GROUP A

Let us begin by looking at Group A. Most of the abilities in this group develop in two clusters. The first, which occurs throughout the first six years of life, fulfills the mind's first three needs (to create stability, to experience input, and to process information). These abilities are vital to the mind's capacity to create an interim understanding of the world. The psychological turbulence that occurs near the end of this period of rapid development is the Oedipal crisis. Once the mind fulfills its needs sufficiently to achieve a stable interim understanding, Group A development wanes and remains relatively dormant for about two decades.

The second burst of Group A ability development occurs optimally in the late twenties and early thirties. That is when the mind, once again fulfilling its need for increased input, develops its capacity to access and process intuitive input. The turbulence caused by this rapid period of development is the midlife crisis (see Chapter 11).

GROUP C

The abilities in Group C are more or less evenly spaced as they emerge. And they continue to develop throughout childhood, adolescence, and youth. One exception to this pattern occurs in late adolescence, when the mind rapidly expands its capacity to comprehend the extended world. The resulting flurry of development to meet the mind's increased need for new concepts causes the psychological turbulence of the identity crisis.

One additional note: I believe that the pattern and duration of ability development in Group C suggest that the commonly held notion that most new development occurs only in childhood is wrong. They also suggest that there is much yet to be learned about the mind's development throughout youth.

The pattern of distribution across age among Group A and Group C abilities is depicted in Figure 10.

Group A *Abilities*	xxxxxxxx			xxxxx
Group C *Abilities*	x x x x x x x x x x xxxxx x x x x x x x			
Life Crisis	Oedipal	Identity		Midlife
Age	0	10	20	30

Distribution of Need Fulfillment in Immaturity
FIGURE 10

Fulfillment of the mind's six basic needs through ability development in all three groups positions the mind to construct a fully correct understanding of the world. With the accomplishment of this milestone, all type-1 ability development ceases.

A Look Back and a Look Ahead

From our bird's-eye view, we can now see that Chapter 6 was actually a description of how Group A abilities form the mind's interim capacity to understand during the first six years of life. And we can see that Chapter 7 was mostly about Group B abilities, whose function is simply to develop new abilities. As we move ahead, we shall see how Group C abilities function throughout immaturity to expand how much of the world the mind can understand.

~ 9 ~

The Path to Maturity

*H*ow does the mind—which in infancy can understand only an infinitesimal portion of the world—expand its capacity to understand? In this chapter we shall look once again—from a somewhat different perspective—at the ratchet-like formula the mind uses to mature.

As you will recall, according to the formula, the mind first expands that portion of the world it experiences psychologically as "real," then develops the abilities needed to understand and deal with the new range. Using this formula repeatedly over the span of psychological immaturity ultimately positions the mind to understand the world at large.

Creating a World That Is "Real"

To illustrate the relationship between range and psychological reality, let us consider Gary, a ninth-grader for whom the idea of college is still not "real." At some point in late adolescence, the range created by Gary's mind will begin to expand to include distant places. When that happens, going to college will take on a presence that was not there earlier.

Gary's mind will then begin to develop the abilities he needs to understand and deal with "college": leaving home, being on his own, preparing for the future, and so on.

The psychologically real world is the only portion of the world the mind is capable of understanding. To the developing person, this portion is stimulating, meaningful, alive. The rest of the world, which must be created through a learning process and retained solely through memory, is remote and lifeless and holds little sustainable interest.

The Maturational Formula: Step 1: Expanding Range

In everyday life an incremental expansion of range may go unnoticed. But in the overall process of psychological maturation, there are four major identifiable stages in range expansion.

Stage 1 extends from birth to about age six—the period during which the mind constructs its ability to create a stable interim understanding of the world. Stage 2 begins at about age six and extends up to the end of adolescence. Stage 3 begins with the onset of youth and lasts until the beginning of the midlife crisis. Stage 4 covers the midlife crisis.

Throughout these stages the mind can expand its range in one or both of two ways: by increasing the types of sensory input it can access from the brain and/or by expanding the portion of the world each form of input covers.

Now let us look more closely at each stage.

STAGE 1: BIRTH TO AGE SIX

At birth the mind's range is virtually nonexistent. Although the infant can physically taste, smell, hear, feel, and see, the mind does not automatically experience all the sensory data that reaches the brain. Over the first few years of life, the child's mind will progressively develop the capacity to access input from each of the first five senses. And by age six the use of all five senses is securely established. In addition, the child has extended range within each form of sensory input until he or she can experience as real the physical world of home and the immediate neighborhood.

STAGE 2: AGE SIX TO THE END OF ADOLESCENCE

Over the next twelve years or so, the child's mind extends that portion of the physical world that registers as real until it encompasses all that can be experienced directly by the five senses. Here, physical contact is an important ingredient in establishing range. For example, it helps to take a child to a new school and let him or her explore it before the first day of class: Doing so gives the child an opportunity to make school psychologically real and enables his or her mind to begin to develop the abilities that will allow the child to adjust.

In adolescence, the mind's range expands to encompass the outlying community—neighboring towns, the nearby beach or mountains. But still, the only part of the world that is psychologically real is the portion that has been directly experienced. (You may have noticed that most adolescents tend to show relatively little interest in national and international issues and rarely read newspapers. That is because "the world out there" is not yet real to them.)

STAGE 3: YOUTH TO THE ONSET OF THE MIDLIFE CRISIS

With the onset of youth, the mind's range expands to include places, subjects, and events well beyond what the adolescent was able to understand. What makes this possible is the mind's added capacity to utilize abstractions to create new range. Now subjects such as college or career, politics, domestic and foreign policy, the role of religion in society, the "rest of my life" must all be dealt with in some competent fashion. To handle this enormous increase in range, the mind needs vast numbers of new abilities, and it is virtually impossible for it to develop these abilities quickly enough to keep up. The resulting deficit precipitates the identity crisis, a protracted period of instability and turbulence.

STAGE 4: THE MIDLIFE CRISIS

Just as the mind in childhood increased its range primarily by adding new forms of perceptual input, the mind at midlife increases its range by adding intuitive input. This results in a dramatic expansion in range. The mind's inability to deal with the new range—along with its inability to process this new type of input—creates the midlife crisis. Once the mind develops the concepts needed to process intuitive input and to understand the added range, the crisis is over.

These four stages of range expansion are depicted in Figure 11.

The Maturational Formula: Step 2: Filling in New Range

The abilities most useful for filling in new range are those Group C abilities that enable the mind to form new concepts. Good, bad, long, short, safe, frightening, near, far, volume, fullness are all such concepts. They portray some part or characteristic of the world. The more of these concepts the mind develops, the more of the world it will understand. Cognitive psychologists have supplied us with the perfect illustration of this phenomenon:

Method of Creating Range:		Direct Experience		Abstracting	
Input:		Five Senses			Six Senses
Stage:	1	2	3	4	
Age:	0	10	20	30	

The Four Stages of Range Expansion in the
Immature Stage of the Life Cycle
FIGURE 11

A teacher places two containers on a table in front of a four-year-old and a seven-year-old. One container is tall and slender, the other short and broad. The tall, slender container is filled to the brim with water. The teacher then pours the water from it directly into the short, broad container, which becomes only partially filled. The teacher asks the children: "Which container had the most water?" The four-year-old says, "The tall, skinny container." The seven-year-old gives the correct answer: "They both had the same amount."

The four-year-old reached his answer using a model based on the concept of fullness. The seven-year-old reached her answer from the correct model, based on the concept of volume. The teacher then tells both children the correct answer—"Each container held the same amount of water"—and asks the question again. This time both children respond correctly. But now the teacher takes the four-year-old aside and emphatically asks, "What is the correct answer?" The four-year-old recants and says, "The tall, skinny one."

This child's level of understanding, based on the concept of fullness, is, at age four, the most advanced psychological concept he has developed to solve this problem. When the child was first told he had given the wrong answer, he simply repeated the right one. Until he develops the concept of volume, the four-year-old may be able to supply the correct answer from memory, but he cannot understand why that answer is correct.

Over time, the mind must develop hundreds of individual concepts to understand even the smallest range. Moreover, it will require thousands, perhaps tens of thousands, of concepts over the course of psychological immaturity to understand the world at large.

Concept Formation During the Four Stages

During immaturity the mind will correctly develop most of the concepts needed to enable the person to understand and deal with an ever-expanding range. But invariably some will be compromised. Each of us grows up with a blend of correctly formed and compromised concepts. Although compromised concepts are not the most favorable development, the existence of a reasonable number poses no particular threat to achieving the goal of psychological maturity. There are, however, several concepts that, if compromised, hold the power to eventually interrupt the implementation of the maturational formula. Should this happen, range expansion—as well as new concept formation—may come to a halt, ending progress along the maturational path.

Critical Concepts During Immaturity

GOOD

The concept of "good" enables the child to begin to value people, ideas, beliefs—various "things"—in the world. This concept is very important, because through its use the young child begins to assign value to a slowly developing sense of self. The experience that "I am good" enables the child to conceptualize himself or herself as "worthy." This, in turn, eventually facilitates the process of centering on oneself as a person, of putting oneself first.

Because successfully negotiating the maturational path requires thousands of steps and years of single-minded commitment—expressed in such ways as becoming proficient at play, doing well in school, succeeding at one's work, and forming effective personal relationships—this level of commitment can be achieved only by those who can put their own development front and center. Because the concept of "good" is fundamental to this orientation, it is an absolute requisite for sustained movement along the maturational path.

The widespread emergence in the 1970s of those in youth who put their own development first produced the so-called Me Generation. Society, unable to see the behavior of a generation of "self-centered kids" from a life cycle perspective, eventually grew convinced that such self-development was simply an undesirable variant of selfishness and self-indulgence. Without the proper map, this behavior was not allowed to "work," and an entire generation ultimately became apologetic merely for continuing to develop along the maturational path.

NO

The concept of "no," formed at about eighteen months of age, is also of great importance. For maturation to proceed correctly, the child must have the time and space to focus on personal development, and "no" is the concept that insulates the child from the intrusiveness of others. By setting limits on the needs and demands of others, "no" helps to give the maturing person the freedom to develop according to the exclusive needs of an internal path.

BODY IMAGE

At birth we cannot conceptualize our own bodies. Although the young child can physically see and feel arms and legs, he or she does not know, psychologically, that these parts exist until they are incorporated into his or her body image. This process of integration will take place one body part at a time, over the entire span of psychological immaturity. The resulting unconscious body image forms out of a collection of type-1 concepts that function in the mind as a "map" of the parts of the body and a schematic of how they work.

During the first six years or so of life, a child develops the body image only of those parts he or she can easily see: hands, arms, chest, stomach, genitals, legs, and feet. The other parts—buttocks, back, spine, internal organs, neck and shoulders, head—will be conceptualized over the remaining three decades of immaturity.

One's body image is central to a sense of being male or female and crucial to a well-formed sense of identity. Completing this collection of unconscious images is essential to the psychological concept that "I am a whole person."

A developed part within a body image serves two functions. First, at the most basic level, it lets the child unconsciously know, for example, that "I have an arm." Second, the development of the image of certain body parts brings added psychological reality.

This principle can be illustrated in the reality that accompanies the development of the sense of having genitals in the male child. This inclusion permits him to operate in the world according to the *principle of sufficiency*. Sufficiency, in this context, means that perfectly acceptable standards exist well short of the extreme. One is thus free from the constant need for perfection, or the need to have the most, the newest, the biggest of anything—needs that may drive people unmercifully and impose impossible standards for performance. (This should not be construed as condoning or promoting mediocrity. Under certain developmentally advanced circumstances—for example, in craftsmanship—only the highest standard may be sufficient.)[1]

A compromised body image in either a male or a female child results in a sense of shame. This, in turn, leads to withdrawal and a subsequent loss of impetus to complete one's trek down the maturational path.

INDEPENDENT ACTION

The concept of independent action is of particular importance. Much has been said about Freud's concept of the Oedipus complex, which holds that a five-year-old boy's unconscious sexual love for his mother conflicts with his alignment with, and fear of, his father. The boy's unconscious fear of castration by the father causes him to abandon his desire for his mother and identify more completely with his father, thus resolving the crisis. Such configurations emerge in the psychoanalytic treatment of men, and the resolution of the Oedipal crisis is a remarkable milestone in the treatment of a neurosis.

According to maturational theory, however, all children are confronted at a much deeper cognitive level with the painful perception that a relationship (frequently experienced as sexual) exists between the mother and father—a relationship that has nothing to do with the child. This realization, initially met with jealousy and rage, is the earliest manifestation of the child's capacity to conceptualize independent action. This crucial step in the development of the mind forms the basis for the child's later understanding that much of what goes on in the world has absolutely nothing to do with him or her. Such knowledge later enables the mind to construct models that are totally grounded in the outside world—devoid of personal references. These models are critical to differentiating fully between inside and outside and, as such, are a requisite for understanding the world correctly.

When the capacity to conceptualize independent action is lacking, one automatically assumes one has—or should have—some personal involvement in all experiences. Thus whereas it is normal for a three-year-old to believe that people having a conversation across the room may be talking about him or her, it is unduly burdensome for a twenty-year-old to create this same self-centered reality. Failure to develop the concept of independent action is the cognitive flaw that causes the common problem called narcissism.

BORROWING FROM ONESELF

As we have seen, in early youth, range increases dramatically to encompass the world at large. Now, for the first time, the mind cannot fill the deficit in the traditional manner—by borrowing from others. As mentioned earlier, the chaos that follows is the identity crisis.

In the mid-1950s, when Erikson first described this crisis, he left unanswered the question of how forming a sense of identity resolved the crisis. I submit that a sense of identity catalyzes the development of the concept "I can borrow from myself."

Instead of filling internal voids with "what I must have from others," one can fill the voids with a sense of "what I can be" and "what I want to become." Self-borrowing thus releases one from the intense need for others and places future maturation increasingly in one's own hands. The resulting understanding that "I can do for myself" enables the person in crisis to relax and settle in to the next phase of the maturational process. With this, the identity crisis is over.

The capacity to self-borrow also enables the person to move forward with a sense of being (psychologically) "singular," and being comfortable in the singular state positions one correctly for the remaining years of intense development. Conversely, the person who remains unduly dependent on borrowing from others continues to have the need to be "coupled," believing it to be the normal state. From this point on, this person will experience intense inner pressure to be in a relationship. This places undue strain on the maturational process, because the person—believing that the psychological presence of others is a permanent state—must continue to rely heavily on outside borrowing.

INTERNAL VOID

Finally we come to the concept of an internal void. In immaturity, the mind usually experiences any deficit as an internal void and responds with a sense of tension. You might recall that the formula of increased range followed by a void in concept formation causes the mind to try to reduce the resulting tension by minimizing the void through negation, or by filling it through borrowing. Obviously, the more the mind can develop its capacity to tolerate a void, the less it will need to depend on borrowing or negation to reduce tension. Tolerating a void enables one to focus on one's own development, an absolute requisite for successfully resolving the upcoming midlife crisis.

The Formula and Relationships

Relationships with others are important to the formula. They supply the context in which the mind can develop new concepts. There are at least four different ways relationships perform this function:

- Forming relationships enables one to secure organizers, which, in turn, effect consolidation. Only when the mind is consolidated can it remain stable—a requisite for most concept formation.
- Relationships provide us with access to a variety of actualizers—people integral to the creation of concepts because they grant permission for abilities to be formed.
- Many relationships provide the opportunity for practicing behavior to take place. As we now know, for the maturing person, engaging in this behavior is a crucial step in the development of all type-1 abilities, including concept formation.
- Finally, relationships act as the context for borrowing. The mind, you will recall, experiences the developmental deficit caused by expansion in range as an internal void, which is associated with tension. Borrowing decreases tension and frees the mind to focus on developing new concepts.

Relationships with other people are not the only kind that facilitate type-1 ability formation. Relationships with oneself, one's job, places, belief systems, and any other ideas or things can also work as organizers or actualizers, or as sources for borrowing.

STAGE 1: RELATIONSHIPS FROM BIRTH TO AGE SIX

Early relationship formation centers on the child's bond with the parents, who, for the first few years, are his or her primary organizers. However, the child's world also includes brothers and sisters, aunts and uncles, toys, pets, and friends. In fact, important relationships can exist with a wide array of items—large, small, animate, inanimate—as long as they are experienced by the child as compatible and stable. For the child, these qualities make something suitable for borrowing.

Relationship abilities—such as the ability to connect, bond, mold, grasp, hold on to, let go of, approach, and leave behind—form patterns of behavior that later become incorporated into one's unique style of getting along with others. Patterns of caring, loving, giving and receiving, patterns of aggression and of physical and sexual expression—all composed of type-1 abilities—add to the child's capacity to relate. These abilities, and hundreds more, will form the core of the child's capacity to find and secure relationships crucial to his or her continued movement along the maturational path.

STAGE 2: RELATIONSHIPS FROM AGE SIX TO THE END OF ADOLESCENCE

Important relationships in this stage enable the child or teenager to continue to fulfill the requirements of a developing mind. Primary relationships with the boy or girl next door or with the family pet are replaced by relationships with teachers, classmates, and teammates. The main impetus is toward forming relationships with others "like me." At this point in life it is easier for the mind to borrow from others who are similar in appearance and who are continuously available. Thus, by midadolescence one's primary relationships are with one's peers.

There is also a marked increase in self-consciousness at this time. This signals the rapidly emerging ability to form a relationship with oneself.

STAGE 3: RELATIONSHIPS FROM YOUTH TO THE ONSET OF THE MIDLIFE CRISIS

In this stage of life, the successful resolution of the identity crisis intensifies the importance of one's relationship with oneself to the point where in mid to late youth it can become the primary relationship in one's life. In fact, self-development increasingly becomes the vehicle through which the person in youth can achieve psychological maturity.

STAGE 4: RELATIONSHIPS IN THE MIDLIFE CRISIS

The midlife crisis is frequently experienced as one's "last chance" to get "on track," to establish one's life correctly in the world. It is, of necessity, a period of great self-absorption, turbulence, and instability. Relationships may be abandoned; careers and goals may be changed. By now each person recognizes that he or she must take charge of solving his or her remaining problems; each person realizes that "no one else has my best interest in mind." Whereas some relationships during this stage are formed with an eye toward later life, many are formed out of needs that will last only briefly. This makes it particularly difficult to form permanent relationships while in the throes of a midlife crisis.

Special Problems Within the Four Stages

There are several special problems that occur during the different stages of range expansion. Although they are not tied specifically to the maturational formula, they do spring from the general development of the mind. The most familiar of these are rebelliousness, alienation, and the problems associated with the midlife crisis.

REBELLIOUSNESS

During Stage 1, maternal and paternal carriers should be retired through the achievement of maternal and paternal constancy. But sometimes they are not correctly retired and are to some degree still used in the day-to-day construction of the adolescent's mind. Now these carriers must be retired in a somewhat different fashion. The adolescent, unconsciously experiencing the existence of these carriers as an impediment to the establishment of a pure sense of identity, will try to drive the parents (parental carriers) out by behaving in a manner totally unacceptable to them. This becomes the adolescent's way of restructuring his or her mind so as not to use parental carriers to maintain dyadic equilibrium. This attempt can last up to several years. But, successful or not, it comes to an end.

ALIENATION

The most familiar problem during youth is *alienation*. Like the oppositional child and the rebellious adolescent, the alienated youth is unconsciously using confrontation to achieve a sequence of developmental steps. But instead of acting against the parents to establish a sense of autonomy or drive out the parental carriers, the alienated youth acts against something in the extended environment—government, society, culture, and so on—to drive out the context carrier.[2] For some, this step is critical to achieving context constancy.

Alienation is developmentally driven action and should not be confused with conscious dissenting responses. Whether it "works" or not, like most symbolic behavior, it is phasic and should pass within a few years.

THE MIDLIFE CRISIS

Another set of problems occurs during midlife. But before entering the chaotic world of the midlife crisis, let us depart momentarily from the mind's march toward maturity and look at the historical roots of the maturational process. By doing so, we can see how humankind has been trying for thousands of years to achieve what we may now be on the brink of accomplishing.

~ 10 ~

Historical Perspective

Ordinarily we think about growing up from the perspective of interactions between a developing person and the world. Development, for instance, is largely a product of adapting to relationships with parents, friends, teachers, to education, to competition, to vast amounts of information, and so on.

But constructing the mind through the use of a psychological technique brings this adaptational model into question. It creates a unique perspective and, at least for me, leads to a very different conclusion about psychological development: Rather than resulting primarily from adaptation to the world, psychological development arises from a preexisting internal path.

If this is true, it means that within each newborn there is a program that, if correctly nurtured, will result in psychological maturity. This is of course analogous to the physically developing embryo, in which at the moment of fertilization of the egg the schematic for all future development of each body part and organ system is in place.[1] Over a span of some nine months, each part and system develops along this path until the physical body achieves wholeness.

119

Data on the developing mind have never suggested that psychological maturation might follow such a format. However, isolating the design of the process of psychological maturation brings the inevitable recognition that psychological change is the result of far more than a simple adaptive response to an ever-more-complex world. The design reveals that our fundamental capacity to understand is assembled out of type-1 abilities, which arise in a predetermined sequence and build to a clear and distinct end point: the capacity to create a fully correct understanding of the world. In other words, the formula for the development of the mind's capacity to create a fully correct understanding of our world—like the format for the development of the body—was set in place at some point in humanity's collective past. But unlike physical development, the gift of automatically achieving this psychological goal was not bestowed. Instead, it has been the charge of each generation to ensure that each successive generation is given the opportunity to develop further along this path.

Looking for Evidence of Movement Along a Path

What evidence would bear out the proposition that over the millennia our species has been slowly but progressively evolving along a preexisting maturational path? I suggest that the evidence must meet three requirements: (1) It must enable us to determine the common levels of psychological maturation within a historical population. (2) It must then show that successive generations achieved more advanced levels of maturation. (3) It must show that such advancement conforms to the characteristics associated with development along the maturational path.

But we are instantly beset by a dilemma, for certainly not everyone in a given population achieves the same level of psychological maturation. There have probably always been a few special individuals who developed well beyond their agemates. Plato, Aristotle, Copernicus, Newton, Einstein all achieved the capacity to think relativistically and so by definition at least attained the life stage of youth. However, such individuals surely reflect the exception. The average person, who would statistically make up the bulk of the general population, presumably achieves a somewhat lower maturational level. A reason for this assumption is readily apparent: Our distant ancestors—oblivious to the existence of the maturational process and with little sense of what "works" developmentally—could scarcely have been expected to give their offspring the type of care and education required to facilitate such extensive development.

Not surprisingly, historical accounts of life cycle patterns seem to bear out this assumption. For most of history, the average person's life cycle reflected a pattern of psychological growth in childhood followed by a permanent commitment—that is, to marriage, childbearing, and work—in the early teenage years. Indeed, as late as the midnineteenth century, a woman who was not married by age sixteen or so ran a serious risk of becoming an "old maid."

Historians with an eye for psychological data generally agree that before this century the most common life cycle profile was childhood followed immediately by adulthood. Although most people presumably achieved physical maturity, they probably did not mature psychologically beyond childhood as a stage of life.

In 1904 psychologist G. Stanley Hall published *Adolescence: Its Psychology and Its Relations to Physiology, Anthropology, Sociology, Sex, Crime, Religion, and Education.* In this work he meticulously described the emergence into the general population of a new type of teenager, documenting for the first time a new stage in the human life cycle.

About Hall's work psychologist Kenneth Keniston explains:

> Hall was clearly reflecting a gradual change in the nature of human development, brought about by the massive transformations of American society in the decades after the Civil War. During these decades, the "working family," where children labored alongside parents in fields and factories, began to disappear; rising industrial productivity created new economic surpluses that allowed millions of teenagers to remain outside the labor force. America changed from a rural agrarian society to an urban industrial society, and this new industrial society demanded on a mass scale not only the rudimentary literacy taught in elementary schools, but higher skills that could only be guaranteed through secondary education. What Hall's concept of adolescence reflected, then, was a real change in the human experience, a change intimately tied to the new kind of industrial society that was emerging in America and Europe.
>
> Today, Hall's concept of adolescence is unshakably enshrined in our view of human life. . . . A stage of life that barely existed a century ago is now universally accepted as an inherent part of the human condition.[2]

This means that whereas the accepted life cycle before 1904 had been childhood followed by adulthood, after the publication of Hall's work it became childhood followed by adolescence followed by adulthood.

In the 1940s new forces again reshaped the essence of America's child-rearing practices. First, better parenting and educational techniques grew out of the insights provided by developmental theory. Second, a new emphasis on higher education arose from the experience of the Great Depression: Parents began to view a college education as the best way to protect their children against the pain and dislocation that accompanies hard economic times. Last, a rapidly advancing technological society required even more education.

By the 1960s Keniston began to study a newly emerging behavior in the student population. Men and women on American college and university campuses—most of them in their late teens and early twenties—were experiencing a profound sense of alienation: toward their educational institutions; toward prevailing social policy; toward society in general. Campus protest was commonplace. The Civil Rights Movement and the opposition to the Vietnam War moved protest off campus and into the streets of America's cities. Student opposition now became a matter of national concern; in June 1970 a Gallup poll cited campus unrest as the nation's main problem.

But according to Keniston, alienated behavior was only one of many far-reaching changes occurring deep within the psyche of this young population. And in the fall of 1970 he published his paper "Youth: A 'New' Stage of Life." In it he concluded that these changes all pointed to the emergence into the human life cycle of a new stage. Keniston writes:

If neither "adolescence" nor "early adulthood" quite describes the young men and women who so disturb American society today, what can we call them? My answer is to propose that we are witnessing today the emergence on a mass scale of a previously unrecognized stage of life, a stage that intervenes between adolescence and adulthood. I propose to call this stage of life the stage of youth, assigning to this venerable but vague term a new and specific meaning. Like Hall's "adolescence," "youth" is in no absolute sense new: indeed, once having defined this stage of life, we can study its historical emergence, locating individuals and groups who have been in "youth" as a stage of life in the past. But what is "new" is that this stage of life is today being entered not by tiny minorities of unusually creative or unusually disturbed young men and women, but by millions of young people in the advanced nations of the world.[3]

As mentioned earlier, Keniston believed that this new stage of life was "optional"—entered by some and circumvented by many. With this belief, he remained generally faithful to the tenet of developmental theory, which holds that the developmental process stops unfolding at the end of adolescence.

Thus, for the second time in a century, interest in the emergence of a new form of behavior led to the discovery of a new stage of life—a discovery that proposed to revise the life cycle by inserting youth between adolescence and adulthood. (See Figure 12.)

Before 1904	Childhood	Adulthood		
1904–1970	Childhood	Adolescence	Adulthood	
1970–	Childhood	Adolescence	Youth	Adulthood

The Historical Evolution of the Stage of Life Model
FIGURE 12

Note again that Keniston proposed a new, subtle, and interesting twist in our understanding of the life cycle when he suggested that a cognitive characteristic defines each life stage. Concrete thinking indicates childhood; abstract thinking indicates adolescence; and relativistic thinking best indicates youth. (See Figure 2.)

Placed in historical perspective, this model suggests that

before the twentieth century most adults in the general population remained psychologically arrested in childhood. Although they continued to grow up physically, their thinking remained concrete or literal. The stages of life in which higher thought forms are constructed simply never occurred—an inference that partially explains the harsh, rigid world that our ancestors constructed for themselves.

Remember too that, historically speaking, the capacity to think abstractly was extended to the general population only within the past century or so. And the capacity for relativistic thought—viewing issues from other frames of reference—became prevalent only over the past thirty years. The timing of this latest change partially accounts for our society's relatively recent willingness to tackle such issues as racial and gender discrimination and gay rights. These issues did not receive so much attention in the past simply because not enough people had the capacity to understand the world from another's point of view.

Another inference that can be drawn from Keniston's work is that adulthood was not, for him, in the strictest sense a stage of life in that it had no underlying and defining cognitive characteristic. From this perspective, adulthood has always acted as a plug, which is stretched as needed to fill the gap between the last described "true" stage of life—whether it be childhood, adolescence, or youth—and the end of the life span. This point will be discussed in greater detail in Chapter 12.

Symbolic Behaviors as Markers

Both Keniston's and Hall's discoveries were by-products of their interest in a newly emerging form of behavior in the general population. For Hall it was the emergence of rebellious behavior into the general teenage population that led to his discovery of adolescence as a stage of life. For Keniston, it was the emergence of alienation among college students that led to his discovery of youth as a life stage.

I believe that the behaviors Hall and Keniston observed were classically symbolic. I also believe that symbolic behavior acts as a reliable marker to identify the unfolding of a specific part of the maturational path: Rebellious behavior in teenagers indicates midadolescence; alienation in college students indicates early youth. In each case, interest in a particular symbolic behavior correctly resulted in the discovery of a new stage of life.

Identifying the emergence of new forms of symbolic behavior is a valuable method of tracking the unfolding maturational path over great spans of time. But in order to function as a reliable marker, symbolic behavior must have four characteristics:

- It must have a unique, recognizable form.
- It must be dramatic in appearance.
- It must point to a specific period in the maturational path.
- And it must have a long enough "life span" for its emergence to be noticed.

For example, even though one's work could be symbolic, its presence throughout immaturity as a general life behavior makes it indistinguishable from work as symbolic behavior. As such, the symbolic behavior of "working" would not qualify as a marker. But rebelliousness and alienation do qualify since they conform on all counts.

Interestingly enough, two additional forms of symbolic behavior have emerged in the general population in the last twenty years. Each qualifies as a marker, and each indicates further movement along the maturational path. One is the practice of running as a form of physical fitness; the other is the midlife crisis.

Running took America by storm in the 1970s. A historically sedentary population of twenty-, thirty-, and forty-year-olds (and occasionally older) suddenly put on baggy shorts and funny-looking shoes and hit the pavement. These men and women (their numbers would eventually swell to 30 million in this country and 100 million worldwide) held a special place in the general population. They were, by and large, highly educated: doctors, bankers, teachers. (By one published account, over half the runners in the New York City Marathon held a master's degree or better.) And, although advanced levels of psychological maturation are in no way limited to any one socioeconomic group, the better educated within any community are usually those who have benefited most from opportunities that promote extensive development.

Dismissed at the time as a fitness fad that would soon go away, running survived, and runners have persisted in stable numbers. Moreover, the fitness boom has expanded to include bicycling, swimming, aerobics, weight training, and so on. All can be symbolic behaviors, pointing to the unfolding of a specific segment of the maturational path in which the capacity for self-development, self-reliance, and the further development of body image are central issues. And I suggest that taken together, all point to the emergence within the general population of midyouth.

The second marker of an unfolding maturational path occurred in the late 1970s and 1980s, when the midlife crisis appeared on the scene. At its most superficial level, the midlife crisis is a cluster of symbolic behaviors. And, like runners, those ''suffering'' from a midlife crisis tend to be better educated and have managed in some way to maintain a maturational orientation in life.

The specifics of the midlife crisis will be examined in the following chapter; for the moment I shall simply suggest that, like running, not only is the emergence of this new

127

form of behavior in the middle-aged population evidence of continued movement along the maturational path but, more specifically, it marks—as unlikely as it may seem—the beginning of our transformation from youth into adulthood. The inference is astounding: Is it possible that even the brightest and most capable among us have not yet achieved psychological maturity? The answer is yes.

One reason for this is that along almost every maturational path a natural moment comes when the confluence of conscious and unconscious personal factors combines with the prevailing sociocultural, family, economic, and religious mores to make a certain amount of maturation seem like the correct amount to qualify one for entrance into life's stream as an adult. I call this the *point of abandonment,* because at this time movement along the maturational path is left in favor of permanent commitments in the adult world. This point, of course, falls short of true psychological maturity—short of that point in the mind's construction that would enable one to create a fully correct understanding of the world.

Every society has a time period that corresponds to the point of abandonment. I call this the *zone of abandonment.* When its members reach this stage of their lives, they are expected to assume adult responsibilities and commitments— the requisites for becoming socially and economically productive (and, up to now, being deemed psychologically mature!). In most advanced societies today, the zone of abandonment lies in early or perhaps midyouth, following the completion of formal education. In the eighteenth century, the zone of abandonment occurred right after puberty.

Maturationally speaking, our species has had a busy past century. During this time the populations of most of the advanced countries of the world have evolved from a general level of maturation that was arrested in childhood to the point at which—for the first time—many are knocking on the door of psychological maturity.

But what about the enormous segment of historical time that predates the emergence of adolescence? Is it possible to date any of the much earlier movement along our maturational path?

Childhood Markers

Documenting the emergence of symbolic behaviors such as rebelliousness, alienation, running, and the midlife crisis is an effective way to date changes in the maturational level of a population over time, but the usefulness of this technique is limited primarily to changes that occur in adolescence and youth. Although symbolic behaviors do emerge in childhood, no one has made the extensive observations of children that would enable us to mark the emergence of such behaviors into the general childhood population.

Theoretically, one juncture in childhood could act as an effective marker if such data were available: the transition from suspended to dyadic equilibrium. This transition brings with it dramatic and distinctive changes in cognitive functioning. Cognitive changes usually go unnoticed in children, but if adults in the general population were arrested in suspended equilibrium, they should show rather distinctive psychological characteristics. These would include the inability to form a clear sense of self; the inability to distinguish inside from outside (which leads to hallucinations and delusions); the inability to think and reason effectively; and even the inability to experience oneself as a person or to know that one possesses a mind.

There is evidence that just such a cognitive transformation emerged abruptly and dramatically at the close of the second millennium B.C. (rather than evolving over the many millennia that constitute the history of humankind). This transformation is the subject of an interesting essay by Princeton

University psychologist Julian Jaynes. In 1976 he published *The Origin of Consciousness in the Breakdown of the Bicameral Mind*.[4] In it he explores the minds of people described in two Greek epic poems: the *Iliad* and the *Odyssey*. The *Iliad*—the story of the Trojan War (and the earlier of the two poems)— is now accepted to have occurred about 1230 B.C. The poem was probably composed shortly after the war and then passed down orally by *aoidoi*—men devoted to creating and transmitting such poetry—until about 900–850 B.C., at which time it was written down.

Jaynes believes that Iliadic man possessed a bicameral mind—an ancient mentality in which the right and left hemispheres of the brain appear to have functioned somewhat independently of each other. Jaynes's selection of the label *bicameral* reflects a neurological emphasis that is not really relevant here. What he observed, however, which is extremely relevant, was that the men and women of the thirteenth century B.C. (and presumably earlier) had no self-awareness and therefore no sense of having a mind, of consciousness, or of being a person. They were similarly unaware of their own thought processes. They openly hallucinated and lived in a delusional state, believing that their actions were designed and directed by gods. Jaynes describes Iliadic man:

> The characters of the *Iliad* do not sit down and think out what to do. They have no conscious minds such as we say we have, and certainly no introspections. It is impossible for us with our subjectivity to appreciate what it was like. (p. 72)

> The Trojan War was directed by hallucinations. And the soldiers who were so directed were not at all like us. They were noble automatons who knew not what they did. (p. 75)

Iliadic man did not have subjectivity as do we; he had no awareness of his awareness of the world, no internal mind-space to introspect upon. (p. 75)

Jaynes then examines the *Odyssey*, a collection of poems about various heroes, created some 100 to 150 years after the *Iliad*. Here he finds a remarkably different mind-set. Jaynes believes the *Odyssey* is evidence for the transformation of bicameral man into the thinking, self-aware man of Classical Greece. In fact, he believes that the *Odyssey* unwittingly describes the breakdown of the bicameral mind, a transformation that was complete in Greece by the sixth century B.C. Jaynes explains: "I am saying—and I find it hard to believe myself—that all this highly patterned legend, which so clearly can be taken as a metaphor of the huge transilience toward consciousness, was not composed, planned, and put together by poets conscious of what they were doing" (p. 277).

Whether or not Jaynes is correct about the neurological basis of the bicameral mind, his conclusion that the mentality of humankind underwent a significant change seems inescapable. Simply put, he has documented the emergence in the general population of a significant event along the maturational path: The mind of the *Iliad* is the mind in suspended equilibrium. But the mind of the *Odyssey* is the mind transforming from suspended to dyadic equilibrium. Remember, it is the movement into dyadic equilibrium that creates consolidation; it is consolidation that creates a sense of inner form; and it is a sense of inner form that creates the sense that "I am a person," the sense of self-consciousness and self-awareness. Moreover, it is the mind's structure in dyadic equilibrium that creates a sense of actually having a mind, and a sense of inside and outside. And it is the mind's processing in dyadic equilibrium that creates both the sense of thinking and the ability to reason.

In his chapter entitled "The Causes of Consciousness," Jaynes seems to suggest four reasons for the "breakdown of the bicameral mind": the mixing of cultures through trade; the migrations of peoples caused by cataclysmic natural disasters; the reduction of an increasingly complicated social structure to writing; and the movement toward larger cities. Although he is somewhat tentative in these suggestions, the forces they—specifically the increased movement into cities—imposed on individual societies are remarkably similar to the forces that preceded the emergence of adolescence and youth into the general population.

Jaynes also looked for evidence that the bicameral mind existed in other cultures. In each culture he examined, he found evidence of an early bicameral period followed by a period of transformation followed by the emergence of the mind familiar to us today. He documents the breakdown of the bicameral mind as a process that began around the thirteenth century B.C. and continued until perhaps the sixth century B.C. throughout the Old World. He suggests that the bicameral mind survived in the Western Hemisphere until the Spanish conquerors arrived in 1532.

If we integrate Jaynes's work with a historical life cycle profile, we see that until the second millennium B.C. even the more civilized of our ancestors coped in a state of suspended equilibrium. Capable of hunting and farming, of banding together in sizable communities, and of waging war, people nonetheless were unable to think effectively, to distinguish clearly inside from outside, to experience self-awareness, or to create any sustained sense of being a person. Amazingly, the zone of abandonment occurred before the accomplishment of dyadic equilibrium.

Was the maturational process present at the origin of our

species? We can never know. What is clear, however, is that shortly before the first millennium B.C., a cross-cultural transformation began from the bicameral to the self-conscious mind. Or, as I need to put it, from suspended to dyadic equilibrium.

The vast majority of humankind floundered in the remainder of childhood as a stage of life for well over 2,000 years—a short time when placed in historical context. Nonetheless, it is understandable that traversing the traps of childhood would take two millennia—especially when one considers the characteristics of concrete-thinking adults, particularly their abhorrence to change.

More recent contributions to human maturation—the demands of a rapidly evolving society, the discovery of the dynamic unconscious, the exercise of individual will in the pursuit of self-realization—have accelerated the rate of maturation, so much so that over the past century we have witnessed more collective movement along our maturational path than has been seen over the entire previous span of human history. The evolution of this process is illustrated in Figure 13.

The inclusion of psychology in history (psychohistory, as it is called) by necessity deals primarily with the aspects of psychological maturation that are open to observation. It is worth mentioning that life cycle profiles that evolve over time are more than newly emerging forms of behavior that, on occasion, indicate the emergence into the general population of a new stage of life. At heart a changing life cycle pattern reflects fundamental advances along the maturational path, and therefore in the construction of the mind's capacity to create a fundamental understanding of our world. Unless one remains mindful of this, psychohistory promotes a behavioral orientation (instead of a maturational orientation) with the misleading conclusion that movement

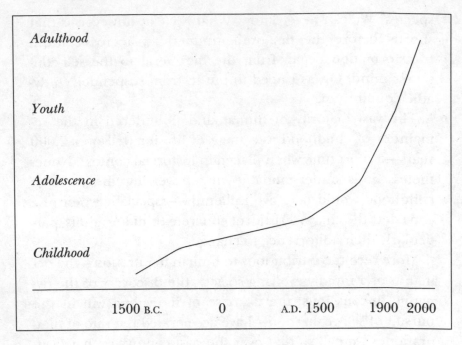

Historical Life Cycle Profile
FIGURE 13

down the maturational path produces solely the emergence of new forms of behavior. In this orientation, the relationship between behavior and the mind's construction is lost. Hence, rebelliousness represents primarily an issue of anger with one's parents; or the identity crisis becomes exclusively a matter of finding out who I am; or the midlife crisis is behavior stemming from our unconscious confrontation with the inevitability of our own death. But these issues are simply symbolic expressions, incorporated into the attempt to continue constructing the fabric of the mind.

Finally, I need to reemphasize that these psychological advances were not accomplished in the classical evolutionary sense. Rather, they reflect movement down a preexisting path—a template every bit as inherent as the physical one that creates the brain, the heart, and the muscles in the arm. Moreover, it is a path whose potential has yet to be fully realized. And if one is to believe the markers in this historical continuum, this potential can be realized with the successful negotiation of the midlife crisis.

~ 11 ~

The Midlife Crisis

A few months after his forty-third birthday, Bob found himself increasingly adrift in a sea of doubt about the direction his professional life was taking. To an outside observer, that life would seem to be successful and fulfilling. An executive in a major manufacturing firm, Bob earned a substantial income and was highly respected by his peers. Yet for some indefinable reason he felt dissatisfied. "I should be doing something more important than this," he told himself.

It was much the same at home. Although he was part of a wonderful family, Bob no longer wanted to share his life with Barbara, the college sweetheart he had married twenty years ago. Their children, now sixteen and seventeen, would soon be leaving home for college, and Bob found himself thinking about divorce. As the months passed, both his wife and his colleagues noticed that Bob was increasingly withdrawn. He was also troubled by unusual impulses, such as wanting to "be open" and wanting to "stop." He fell into more and more frequent fits of moodiness, of irritability, of wanting to be left alone. He fantasized about having an affair. From time to time he longed to start over.

In more stable moments, Bob thought about his late parents, wishing he had had a better, more loving relationship with them. And as he grew increasingly introspective, Bob for the first time began to think about his own mortality. Looking deeper into himself than ever before, Bob became convinced—in a way that no one around him could understand—that somehow his whole life had been wasted. He was equally convinced that the next few weeks or months represented his last chance to pursue a path that would lead to true happiness, meaning, and fulfillment.

Bob is well into his midlife crisis!

The Anatomy of the Midlife Crisis

The midlife crisis is the third and last of the normal crisis periods that occur on the journey to psychological maturity. It is precipitated by a combination of two factors.

First, during mid- to late youth, the mind's range expands to include intuitive input. (Here, I want once again to emphasize that I am using *intuition* and *intuitive input* quite differently from the popular usage. Most people ordinarily think of intuition as a valuable—albeit indefinable or mysterious—way to understand or perceive a subject. Maturational theory, however, defines intuition as a basic form of sensory input that conveys a specific and unique type of information about a subject—just as hearing conveys how a subject sounds, or seeing conveys how it looks. With intuition, the information conveyed pertains to how a subject changes over time.) The problem with the addition of intuitive input during the midlife crisis is that it produces more data than the mind can understand and deal with. As time passes, the mind becomes overwhelmed by the increased data.

The second factor that precipitates the midlife crisis is the limitation of the S_1 carrier—the immature mind's workhorse for processing information. As you will recall, the S_1 carrier is a special type-1 ability that, among its other functions, uses input from the first five senses to create an understanding of a subject. But the S_1 carrier cannot effectively make use of intuitive input. This causes the mind to become disoriented—a hallmark of the midlife crisis. The problem will be resolved when the S_1 carrier is replaced by the *S_2 carrier,* which is designed to process input from all six senses.

In sum, the midlife crisis begins with the onset of a sudden increase in range brought about by the addition of intuitive input. The crisis evolves as the mind replaces the S_1 carrier with the S_2 carrier. And it ends when the mind develops the stable capacity to process input from all six senses using the S_2 carrier.

Back to Bob

To help us understand the symptoms of the midlife crisis, let us return for a moment to the maturational formula the mind uses to increase how much of the world it can understand. The first step, as we know, is to expand range. Bob's moodiness, irritability, and desire to be left alone all reflect a new range that extends not only outward but inward, into himself. The unusual thoughts and feelings he may now be experiencing—such as wanting to "stop" or to "be open," or wanting to "get under" some part of himself, or "wanting out"—are most likely outward expressions of the inner process.

Without a maturational map, such thoughts and sensations can be alarming, even frightening. But in reality all these sometimes seemingly bizarre "symptoms" reflect steps or adjustments the mind is making as it expands its capacity to include intuitive input. All are a normal part of the midlife crisis.

For the next several months, or even several years, Bob will continue to struggle with the idea of his own death, including the question of life after death. Within the context of the midlife crisis, however, this struggle actually reflects the progressive disassembling of the mind as the S_2 carrier replaces the S_1 carrier.

More straightforward, perhaps, may be Bob's concern about his work. Commitments made in early youth frequently do not work out. After all, it is difficult to know at that point in the life cycle where one's true talents and enduring interests lie. It logically follows, then, that commitments made so early would be difficult to sustain.

Bob's deteriorating relationship with his wife, Barbara, is a bit trickier to assess. This too could be a case of premature commitment. Perhaps their relationship was based primarily on her role as an organizer, or an actualizer, or as someone who possessed characteristics he needed to borrow. Then, as his development proceeded, Bob's dependency on outside sources became less compelling. Perhaps now he requires a different, more sustainable basis for a relationship. If his relationship with Barbara never took this next essential step, there may be little left to hold them together. Or perhaps his disillusionment with the marriage reflects a greater sense of simply wanting to start over: an attempt to clean house and "remove the mistakes," so to speak, from his life and from himself.

To be perfectly honest, at this point Bob probably cannot separate one issue from another. In time the marriage crisis will play itself out. If the underpinnings of a solid relationship exist, if over the years their love and respect for each other have flourished, and if they can weather this midlife storm, then the marriage should survive.

Bob's sense that this is his last chance to step onto a path leading to true happiness may be common to every midlife crisis. This is a thinly veiled metaphor for one's last chance to become mature. And it is probably true. In reality, it is Bob's first, last, and only chance to become truly mature. The failure to resolve correctly his midlife crisis will leave Bob in a permanent state of psychological immaturity.

"What Is the Matter with Me?"

Our excursion into Bob's midlife crisis is designed to show how many of the classic symptoms of the crisis are related to changes taking place within the developing mind. But there is yet another group of symptoms unique to the midlife crisis. They can mimic various brain disorders, or even early senility. They can last from a few days to several weeks or months. Forgetfulness, loss of long-term memory, inability to articulate words, physical and psychological clumsiness—all reflect changes occurring deep within the mind. Some of the effects can be rather severe. One of my patients, at about age fifty, was convinced she had developed early Alzheimer's disease. But over many months, symptoms associated with the midlife crisis mercifully disappear.

In sum, the midlife crisis is much more than a collection of strange and bothersome symptoms. It is the transformation of a mind able to use only five senses to create an interim understanding of the world into a mind able to access all six senses to construct a fully correct understanding of the world. Believe it or not, it is a time when mostly good things happen.

Taking the Final Steps

The midlife crisis is immaturity's homestretch. Although most of the maturational work required to become mature has already been done, critical final steps remain. They will determine whether the mind's transformation from immaturity to maturity does indeed take place.

These steps revolve around fulfilling the mind's six basic maturational needs. As you will recall, each represents an area of functioning integral to the construction of the system the mind uses to understand. These six needs are to create stability, to experience all input, to process information, to develop new psychological abilities, to form concepts, and to form relationships.

As each of these needs is fully met—an end point I call *basic competency*—the mind no longer requires additional type-1 abilities in that area. Toward the end of the midlife crisis, the mind will have fulfilled all its needs—that is, it will have achieved basic competency in all six areas of functioning. At that point the mind is positioned to create a fully correct understanding of the world and the person has become psychologically mature.

Let us now look in more detail at how the mind achieves basic competency in each of the six areas of functioning.

1. THE CAPACITY TO CREATE STABILITY

The most dramatic symptoms of the midlife crisis are associated with the mind's need to remain stable. In order to reach basic competency in this area of functioning, the mind must somehow manage to achieve stability without the use of the S_1 carrier—its centerpiece for stability throughout immaturity. This is because the S_1 carrier, which cannot process intuitive input, must be "changed out" for the S_2 carrier. This gap between the dismantling of one stabilizing system and the installation of another produces a period of great instability. To understand how this transition plays havoc with the mind, let us return to Bob.

Since early childhood Bob's mind has functioned primarily through the use of the S_1 carrier. It has served him diligently throughout immaturity: effecting consolidation to keep the mind stable; aligning input from the first five senses with the capacity to process information; and acting as a starting point in the process of thinking. Then, in midyouth, in order to be able later to process intuitive input, Bob's mind begins the slow process of developing a replacement for the S_1 carrier.

At some point during the midlife crisis—before the S_2 carrier is fully in place—the mind will begin to retire its S_1 carriers. As this happens, Bob is caught between two stabilizing systems: one that uses consolidation to effect stability and one that does not.

Without the full benefit of the consolidating effect of the S_1 carrier, and with the S_2 system of stability still not in place, Bob's mind begins to deconsolidate. The deconsolidation leads to the loss of his sense of inner form and with it the loss of the all-important understanding that "I am a person." As Bob spends more and more time in an increasingly deconsolidated state, he is beset by the belief that he is going to die. I suggest that in midlife the struggle with one's mortality is entirely the result of the progressive retirement of S_1 carriers and the subsequent loss of a sense of inner form. Once the mind completes the changing-out process and is securely established in maturity, the mortality issue disappears.

Instability also causes Bob to be intermittently disoriented. Disorientation in midlife is expressed as being unable to "get a fix" on anything. One day Bob wants to remain married; the next he is ready to go out the door. One day he wants to escape to the mountains and become a ski instructor; the next he is opting for the security of his current job. One day Bob can't string a sentence together; the next he is relatively articulate.

By the end of the midlife crisis, the S_2 carrier becomes the mind's functional centerpiece. Consolidation is no longer essential for the mind to remain stable, because it can hold on to the understanding that "I am a person" through the process of self-experience. Also, outside organizers are no longer required for stability, making the mind of maturity self-stabilizing. This is a state I call *independent equilibrium.*

Thus, the mind, late in the midlife crisis and with its newfound capacity to remain stable from within, has achieved basic competency in this area of functioning.

2. THE CAPACITY TO EXPERIENCE ALL INPUT

We know that the mind does not automatically experience all the sensory data that reaches the brain; it must first construct the capacity to do so. Throughout childhood, adolescence, and most of youth, the mind can access only input conveyed to the brain through the five perceptual senses. The capacity to access intuitive input does not begin in earnest until early youth. But over the course of the midlife crisis—if all goes well—the mind will become competent in its capacity to experience intuitive input. It thereby fulfills its second maturational need: to be able to experience all input.

3. THE CAPACITY TO PROCESS INFORMATION

Like the S_1 carrier, the S_2 carrier "secures" thoughts within the mind. Also like the S_1 carrier, it acts as a starting point in the process of thinking. Unlike its counterpart, however, thoughts secured to the S_2 carrier are experienced by the mind as a "whole." Thus, the thought process of immaturity, in which the part is expanded to the whole, is reversed: The whole is created first, and the parts are then filled in. (I shall clarify this elusive concept in Chapters 12 and 14.) The mind, now able to process information from the whole to the part, has achieved basic competency in this area of functioning.

(See Figure 14 for a review of the S_2 carrier and its role in the mind's first three areas of functioning.)

4. THE CAPACITY TO DEVELOP NEW
PSYCHOLOGICAL ABILITIES

You may recall that in immaturity each type-1 ability is developed through a five-step sequence. The newly emerging ability is first experienced as a need. Then it must be practiced and actualized before it can be integrated as an active component in the mind. (See Figure 9.)

You may also remember that this sequence requires other people to function as actualizers. Their role is first to understand and then to grant permission for a newly developing ability to be established. In psychological immaturity, then, there is great dependency upon others in developing the mind.

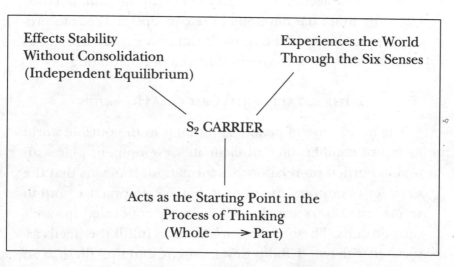

Effects Stability
Without Consolidation
(Independent Equilibrium)

Experiences the World
Through the Six Senses

S_2 CARRIER

Acts as the Starting Point in the
Process of Thinking
(Whole ⟶ Part)

*The Role of the S_2 Carrier in the Mind's
First Three Areas of Functioning*
FIGURE 14

During youth the developing person increasingly experiments with understanding his or her own needs. This process comes to a natural conclusion toward the end of the midlife crisis with the fully developed capacity to recognize that "I, myself, best understand how to facilitate my own development," and, by extension, "I understand my own needs and no longer require permission (actualization) from anyone else." Free at last from the need to depend on others to make the maturational process work, the developing person becomes *self-actualizing*. From this point on, the mind is capable of developing psychological abilities without outside help. This transformation establishes the mind as *self-developing*. As such, it has achieved basic competency in its capacity to develop new psychological abilities.

5. THE CAPACITY TO CREATE CONCEPTS

At the beginning of the midlife crisis, with the inclusion of intuitive input, the mind changes the way it experiences the whole of a subject. And toward the end of the midlife crisis, when the mind has developed the concepts it needs to process and understand the whole it can now experience, it has reached basic competency in this area of functioning.

6. THE CAPACITY TO FORM RELATIONSHIPS

The mind's use of people and things in the outside world to secure equilibrium and facilitate development places an undue burden on relationship formation. It means that the need for organizers, the need to borrow, to practice, and to secure actualizers are all unconsciously concealed in one's relationships. These *symbolic relationships* fulfill the needs associated with type-1 ability development, and they do so as an indistinguishable part of daily life. For instance, when Bob married Barbara, he had no sense that there were underlying

developmental components in their relationship that contributed to his belief that he wanted to spend the rest of
his life with her. But as maturational needs change, earlier
symbolic links within a relationship begin to break down;
the need to move on to a more appropriate relationship
emerges.

As a practical matter, embedding maturational needs in
relationship formation is not a problem in childhood and
early adolescence, when most of life is spent in the service of
developing the mind. But by late adolescence an interest in
having a life separate from maturational needs emerges. Yet as
long as type-1 abilities continue to develop, relationships will
be held hostage to the needs of the immature mind. Adding to
this conflict is the fact that there is no effective way to tease out
the influence of the needs of the developing mind so that one
can comfortably take at face value one's interest in and feelings for another person. For the developing person, from
childhood through the end of youth, the presumption must
be that each new relationship is fundamentally symbolic.

But at the end of the midlife crisis, when type-1 ability formation ceases, the need to borrow and to secure organizers
is outgrown. For the first time, relationship formation is free
from the needs of the immature mind. Now relationships
can be taken at face value.

The development of this capacity to form exclusively *conventional relationships* marks the accomplishment of basic
competency in this line of maturation.

Ending the Midlife Crisis

Reaching basic competency in all six areas of functioning
positions the mind to understand the world using input from
all six senses. This new positioning creates the belief that "I

am now fully able to engage the world," a realization that brings the sense of crisis to a close. We can understand the difference this makes in everyday life by looking at how the mind functions in psychological maturity.

~ 12 ~

Psychological Maturity

*T*he dawning of psychological maturity brings changes within the mind that cause a person to view the world in a different light and from a new set of perspectives. Everything around may look, sound, and feel the same; but the basis for understanding these sights, sounds, and feelings is subtly different. The state of psychological maturity is marked by four major changes:

- The mind now processes input from six senses instead of five
- Aspects of knowledge and experience, originally grounded in the structures of the immature mind, are now grounded in the structures of the mature mind. As a result, the bases for such phenomena as experiencing oneself as a person, distinguishing inside from outside, and experiencing God assume their mature and perhaps final form
- Relationships are no longer symbolic and can be taken at face value
- One's maturational goal—one's primary mission—shifts from becoming psychologically mature to actualizing one's potential in the world

Let us look at how each of these changes manifests itself in our lives.

Processing Input from All Six Senses

Over the span of the midlife crisis, the mind has developed the type-1 abilities it needs in order to fully experience and process intuitive input. But what, specifically, does intuitive input enable the mind to experience that the other five senses do not? And once this new input is experienced, how does it alter our understanding of a subject? Does it simply augment it as, say, knowing an elephant's size, shape, and texture enhances our understanding of that animal? Or does intuitive input *fundamentally change* the way we understand a subject, as the Copernican theory changed how we must understand the universe? The answer is, of course, that intuitive input alters our fundamental understanding of a subject.

How the five perceptual senses contribute to the mind's understanding of a subject is obvious. Each is unique and easily demonstrated. Intuition similarly provides the mind with unique information, and even though how it does this is not so readily apparent, its contribution to the mind's capacity to understand is clearly discernible. Intuitive input alters the way the mind functions in three areas: It enables the mind to (1) envision a different "whole"; (2) conceptualize fundamental design; and (3) process nonlinear sequences. Let's now look at each of these functions individually.

INTUITIVE INPUT AND ENVISIONING A DIFFERENT WHOLE

To understand how intuitive input enables the mind to envision a different whole, let us take as an illustration the subject of this book, psychological maturation. By doing so, we can see how the whole created by maturational theory differs from the whole of developmental theory. The latter, based as it is on concepts formed without the full use of intuitive input, holds that psychological maturity occurs in one's late teens or early twenties. To my knowledge, no scientist has ever suggested that the onset of psychological maturity normally should occur in one's early thirties. *But new information supplied by intuitive input changes our fundamental understanding of the whole (psychological maturation).* The additional input reveals that one does not become mature until the early thirties because becoming mature rests on constructing the mind's capacity to create a fully correct understanding of a subject—a task that takes about three decades to accomplish. So we see that developmental theory creates one whole, whereas maturational theory creates another.

Most any subject can be framed as a whole. The same rule applies: Six senses change the whole. This means, for instance, that our understanding of subjects that constitute the political, social, and behavioral sciences, as well as the humanities, should change dramatically with the addition of intuitive input.

I call the whole created through the use of all six senses a *dynamic singularity.* This replaces the whole created by only five senses. Hence, the concept of immaturity as that part of the life cycle in which the mind is developing its capacity to construct a fully correct understanding of the world is a dynamic singularity. It is a whole that was created with input from all six senses. Conversely, the concept of immaturity as that part of the life cycle in which a person is developing the capacity to engage responsibly in the world is not a dynamic singularity, because it is created through the use of only the first five senses.

INTUITIVE INPUT AND CONCEPTUALIZING
FUNDAMENTAL DESIGN

Over the course of the midlife crisis, the mind develops the capacity to discern the inherent structure, or *fundamental design,* of a dynamic singularity. For example, the fundamental design of immaturity centers on the construction of the system the mind uses to create an interim and then fully correct understanding of the world. The elements of this fundamental design include the parts, the principles through which these parts function together, and a sense of the maturational path central to the construction of the mind. Thus, concepts such as input, equilibrium, processing, and so on frame and describe the fundamental design of the immature phase of the human life cycle.

INTUITIVE INPUT AND PROCESSING NONLINEAR SEQUENCES

The immature mind normally thinks in straightforward, one-step-at-a-time sequences: heat water hot enough and it will boil; or, the more we study, the more we learn. Scientists refer to these progressive steps as *linear sequences.* But upon closer inspection, we can see that most change in the world does not occur in a linear way. More often, it is a highly complex process, in which change in one part of a system creates change in other parts, which in turn further alters the first part.

In the developing mind, for instance, a change in equilibrium will affect all other areas of functioning. These succeeding changes further affect equilibrium by creating, say, anxiety and a sense of instability. And when the sense of instability affects the mind's equilibrium, we are back to square one. We refer to these complex patterns of change as *nonlinear sequences.*

James Gleick writes of the difficulties created in science by nonlinear change:

> They were nonlinear, meaning that they expressed relationships that were not strictly proportional. Linear relationships can be captured with a straight line on a graph. Linear relationships are easy to think about: the more the merrier. Linear equations are solvable, which makes them suitable for textbooks. Linear systems have an important modular virtue: you can take them apart, and put them together again—the pieces add up.
>
> Nonlinear systems generally cannot be solved and cannot be added together. In fluid systems and mechanical systems, the nonlinear terms tend to be the features that people want to leave out when they try to get a good, simple understanding.[1]

Despite the complexity of nonlinear change, we live in a world in which it is the rule, not the exception. Some of the difficulty we face in understanding this change is that the immature mind is not structured to think in nonlinear terms. We must first, as best we can, reduce nonlinear change into one or more easily understood linear sequences.

For the mind to be able to understand nonlinear change directly, it must have access to intuitive input. Although it is still unclear exactly how this type of input does what it does, it is clear that it supplies a special kind of information—the missing ingredient, if you will—critical to the mind's ability to experience the whole, to discern fundamental design, to track change, and therefore to solve nonlinear problems correctly.

I find it profoundly significant that, unlike the immature mind, the mind of maturity seems naturally designed to consider and understand nonlinear relationships. It does this by employing the S_2 carrier, which, you will recall, processes information by starting with the whole and filling in the parts. This characteristic of the S$_2$ carrier dovetails perfectly with the task at hand, because the key to nonlinear understanding is the ability to comprehend change in terms of how parts relate to the whole.

Using the S$_2$ carrier, the mind processes nonlinear problems by forgoing the continuous understanding of how changing parts affect other (changing) parts and instead focusing on the effect of changing parts on the whole. For instance, during psychological maturation, it is next to impossible to describe the unfolding links or sequences between the development of, say, psychological equilibrium and the development of the capacity to form relationships. (Both are parts of the whole: the capacity to understand.) As one tries to follow the cascade of effects, each affecting the others, the mind becomes overwhelmed. But the sense of being overwhelmed quickly disappears when, instead of relating the part to the part, one relates the part to the whole. It is then relatively simple to grasp the relationship between the development of equilibrium (the part) and the development of the capacity to understand (the whole), or between the development of the capacity to form relationships (the part) and the development of the capacity to understand (the whole).

NONLINEAR THINKING AND ADULTHOOD

Up to now the term *adulthood* has functioned as a plug in our understanding of the life cycle. That is, it has had no cognitive underpinning to qualify it as a true stage of life. Instead, adulthood has merely filled the space between the last discovered stage of life and the end of the life span. Before G. Stanley Hall's discovery of adolescence, adulthood spanned the life cycle from childhood on. The discovery of adolescence pushed adulthood a decade ahead, and the discovery of youth pushed it ahead a few more years.

I suggest that *adulthood* is a true stage of life and that the capacity for nonlinear thinking is the psychological underpinning that best defines this stage of life. And perhaps, most remarkably, as the twentieth century comes to a close, adulthood—in its psychological form—is a newly emerging stage of life.

If an adult was just a bit more knowledgeable than a person in youth—as, say, a person with a Ph.D. is to one with a master's degree—then the accomplishment of psychological adulthood would not be of much value. But recognizing adulthood as the stage of life in which the mind has established the capacity for nonlinear thinking is of great significance. According to maturational theory, this capacity enables an adult to construct natural solutions in a nonlinear world. If my view is correct, adulthood is much more than a newly discovered stage of life. It is an accomplishment that enables the mind to understand the world in new and different ways. (This subject will be explored further in Chapter 14.)

Intuitive Input and Understanding the World

The capacity to utilize intuitive input to envision the whole, to conceptualize fundamental design, and to think nonlinearly now positions the mature mind to create a fully correct understanding of the world. Here the term *fully correct* refers to the capacity to experience and process input from all six senses.

The value of a fully correct understanding is that it enables one to isolate and then think about certain subjects correctly. This, in turn, enables one to create solutions that work. This does not mean that the mature person automatically understands subjects correctly. It means only that he or she is psychologically positioned to do so.

PSYCHOLOGICAL STRUCTURE AND A
FULLY CORRECT UNDERSTANDING OF THE WORLD

In immaturity the structure of dyadic equilibrium conveys meaning the mind experiences as knowledge about the world. In Chapter 6 I offered several examples of the kinds of knowledge imparted to the mind through the structure of dyadic equilibrium: a sense of self, a sense of inside and outside, a sense of God, and so on. But with the onset of maturity, dyadic equilibrium has given way to independent equilibrium. To illustrate how the mind adjusts when the structural basis for such knowledge no longer exists, let us return to two examples mentioned earlier: a sense of self and a sense of God.

A Sense of Self

In immaturity the five perceptual senses do not convey enough information to enable the mind naturally to construct the knowledge called a sense of self. Instead, this awareness is tied to the experience of form, which itself is a consequence of consolidation in dyadic equilibrium. For some two and a half decades this method of constructing a sense of self is sufficient. But by the end of the midlife crisis, because the mind no longer uses S_1 carriers, dyadic equilibrium no longer exists. Consequently, all knowledge tied to this structure disappears. If you will remember, earlier in life, whenever the sense of self begins to dissolve, a person's very existence comes into question. The person begins to feel the impending threat of ceasing to exist, or even that he or she is about to die.

Fortunately, when the sense of self begins to wane in the

midlife crisis, a new basis for the knowledge of a sense of self emerges. Now the mind—capable of self-experience through the use of all six senses and capable of using the S_2 carrier to create a new sense of the whole—creates a sense of self just as it creates other types of experiences: through the routine processing of sensory input. For the mature mind, then, reality becomes "I exist because I can experience myself."

A Sense of God

In dyadic equilibrium, we observed that part of one's sense of God is also a function of the structure of the mind. Specifically, God is experienced as being beyond all form (S_1 carriers). But, because thoughts about God are attached to the last developed S_1 carrier, we automatically attribute the characteristics of that carrier to our experience of God. Thus, a person who uses maternal carriers to secure dyadic equilibrium will experience God as maternal. A person who uses paternal carriers to secure equilibrium will experience God as "God the Father." And a person who uses model carriers to secure dyadic equilibrium will experience God as a God of mercy, compassion, love, wisdom, and so on. This knowledge, built into our psychological structure, serves as the starting point from which religion must build.

As one moves into independent equilibrium and S_1 carriers disappear, the experiences of God associated with their use similarly disappear. In other words, the psychological basis for the knowledge that God is the father, or that God is a God of wisdom, compassion, and love, no longer exists. God, of course, may still be any or all of these. But from this point on, because the structure of the immature mind is no longer a contributing factor in one's concept of God, such knowledge must originate solely from outside sources and be maintained entirely on faith.

In maturity, the S_2 carrier acts in a similar fashion to impart knowledge about the fundamental nature of God. Once the S_2 carrier is in place, it is the actualization of potential that is experienced as the realization of God.[2] Thus, at least to some extent, knowledge of God remains grounded in the structure of the mature mind.

Taking Relationships at Face Value

In immaturity relationships are frequently tied to the ever-changing needs of the developing mind and, as such, are likely to be symbolic. But in maturity, when symbolic engagement is no longer a part of everyday functioning, relationships can be taken at face value. Other people remain important to one's life, but they are no longer critical to the integrity of the mind.

Personal relationships in maturity are formed on the principle of "fit," an amorphous blend of characteristics such as compatible personalities, talents, interests, temperaments, and goals as well as such vague but important concepts as physical, sexual, and intellectual chemistry. This allows individuals to join for reasons that will help them attain truly satisfying, mutually fulfilling lives, not primarily to facilitate each other's developmental process. Being able to take relationships at face value makes maturity the right time to commit to permanent relationships.

The Need to Become Mature Yielding to Actualizing One's Potential in the World

Since birth, the mind has obeyed the dictates of a single preemptive drive—to create a fully correct understanding of the world. Shifting interests, numerous symbolic relationships, multiple periods of crisis—all attest to a compelling force bent on achieving maturity. With the mind now positioned to understand the world correctly, it increasingly attends to developing those abilities a person needs to actualize his or her potential in the world. From this point on, the mind's development continues through the construction of type-2 abilities, a process much richer in scope and depth than type-1 development. Rather than driving the mind toward the next step along the maturational path, type-2 development unlocks the full potential inherent in the human mind.

The Positioning of Maturity

Maturity positions each of us to enter the world with the capacity to understand. However, the capacity to understand does not guarantee understanding—it only equips us with the psychological tools to do so. And the capacity to understand does not guarantee success—it only gives us a chance to succeed.

Psychological Development in the Real World

I have presented a model of the life cycle as it would unfold under ideal circumstances. Sadly, the real world does not yet provide the maturing person with such circumstances, and psychological development almost never occurs in such unimpeded fashion. Let us look next at how the bumps, glitches, and derailments of everyday life create detours along the maturational path.

Part III

~~~

~ 13 ~

Detours on the Path to Maturity

Although the inborn impetus toward psychological maturity is a powerful, driving force, the long path toward that goal is strewn with roadblocks and detours. The development of each new type-1 ability presents yet another opportunity for maturation to go astray. True, most compromised abilities offer little threat to the overall integrity of the developing mind. But a few abilities, compromised in just the right—or wrong!—way, can change the course of maturation. In so doing, they can prematurely foreclose the opportunity to become psychologically mature.

So far I have portrayed psychological maturation mostly as an unfaltering progression: type-1 abilities always developing in "pure" form; the availability of suitable borrowing; negation that is never excessive; and the models that invariably support and promote movement along the maturational path. But this ideal progression never happens. Many type-1 abilities are compromised in formation because borrowing doesn't work, or because negation becomes excessive and restricting, or because our models steer us down blind alleys from which there may be no escape.

In this chapter, we shall look at the detours and roadblocks associated with psychological maturation. Most of them fall into two categories: those associated with establishing dyadic equilibrium, and those having to do with staying on the maturational path.

Detour 1:
Failing to Fully Establish Dyadic Equilibrium

It seems reasonable to assume that all children are born with the potential to establish their minds correctly in dyadic equilibrium. The most serious threat to this accomplishment is the mind's failure to develop S_1 carrier configuration that will secure it in a stable form of dyadic equilibrium throughout the long span of psychological immaturity. (This should happen by about age six.)

You may recall that there are five S_1 carriers that secure the mind in dyadic equilibrium by consolidating individual abilities. They are the context carrier, the maternal carrier, the self carrier, the paternal carrier, and the model carrier. Over the course of early childhood, the mind should outgrow the need to use two of these carriers—the mother and father carriers—to effect consolidation. The failure to retire both of these creates two problems. The first is functional: When the mind continues to need early childhood carriers to maintain psychological stability, the mother, the father, or a mother/father substitute continues to operate as organizers. Thus there may be a need to remain in certain relationships for the inappropriate need of staying consolidated.

The second problem is developmental. The optimal time to accomplish constancy—the so-called critical period—has now passed. The remedial component of the maturational process still tries to fix the problem by using close relationships with other people to develop maternal or paternal constancy. However, the mind no longer is capable of fully accomplishing this complex task. The resulting configuration is a *neurosis*.

In a neurosis the mind's developmental struggle is hampered by divided, conflicting goals. On the one hand, the maturational process is working to accomplish the kind of type-1 ability formation appropriate to an expanding life. On the other, the remedial component of the process is trying to achieve the maternal or paternal constancy that was not achieved earlier, so the mind can be correctly established in dyadic equilibrium. We thus have two types of development going on simultaneously: one appropriate to the maturational path, the other, a rerun of early childhood. In such a case, the drive to establish the mind correctly in dyadic equilibrium will be preemptive, because the mind's need to be stable is greater than its need to be mature.

The neurotic person, therefore, must continue to use relationships chiefly for the purpose of developing psychological stability, and then try to make that stability permanent by achieving constancy. Sometimes the mind can accomplish such a task. Most of the time it cannot. By the third decade of immaturity, these two sets of developmental needs overload the maturational process. At some point there is simply too much unfinished business, and the neurotic person begins to settle for the stabilizing effect of a relationship. As this happens, he or she drifts into a state of permanent dependency, opting for a relationship of convenience over continued movement along the maturational path. This reassuring "pod" provides the essential creature comforts in a psychological configuration that will permanently "take two to make one." Any chance of achieving psychological maturity now begins to dissipate, as the mind's capacity to construct itself grinds to a halt under the weight of tasks it cannot achieve.

Detour 2:
Not Adhering to the Maturational Path

Sustaining psychological maturation is no easy task. It means struggling with difficult emotions, tolerating psychological pain, and overcoming unconscious fears while steadfastly adhering to the maturational path. Steering this maturational process is much like driving a car down a narrow, winding road through mountainous terrain. In order to keep moving ahead safely, the driver has to stay in alignment with the demands of the road—the curves, bumps, grades.

CONCEPTS THAT PROMOTE ALIGNMENT

There are two concepts the mind must develop in order to maintain the correct alignment between the developmental process and the maturational path. They are the concepts "I am good" and "I am responsible for my life." These concepts work together to promote self-development, while a sense of uncertainty about one's goodness, coupled with a sense that "others are responsible for my life," compels one to look outward for solutions to inner maturational problems. Under this latter condition, alignment with one's maturational path is unsustainable, and the ability to recognize and respond to one's own developmental needs is eventually lost.

CORRECT MODELS PROMOTE ALIGNMENT

Models that correctly convey the inherent design of the maturational process enable us to place ourselves and others correctly on our respective maturational paths. They allow us to put behavior in maturational perspective. They tell us what we need to know to nurture and expedite movement along the path. For example:

- The primary goal of parenting—from a maturational point of view—should be to nurture the steps that lead to parental constancy and to the establishment of the mind in a stable state of equilibrium.

- Rebelliousness during the teenage years is not rebelliousness for its own sake, but rather for the purpose of correctly developing the mind. Placing rebelliousness in this maturational perspective does not end the rebelling, but it does create a framework that can facilitate the development of the mind while reducing the destructive component of the behavior.

- Throughout immaturity, guilt is a consequence of failing to live up to internal models. In order to alleviate the discomfort from the guilt, the most frequent solution is to alter the behavior causing the guilt. However, frequently the correct response—maturationally speaking—is to change the models, not the behavior.

  For example, Michelle experienced extreme feelings of guilt when she contemplated ending a marriage she believed was a mistake to begin with. To avoid feeling guilty, she had two choices: She could stay in the marriage or change her model "Till death do us part." For a while she stayed in the marriage, trying to find areas of mutual interest with her husband and working on developing better communication skills. However, nothing she tried made the union "right," and still the guilt prevailed. It wasn't until Michelle was able to change her model that she was released from a marriage that could never have worked.

- During the second decade of life one needs to become primarily self-developing. This accomplishment promotes taking control of one's own maturational process. And because maturity is much too difficult a goal to reach by happenstance, it is difficult to imagine sustained psychological growth without this orientation.

Correct modeling in these and many other areas enables one to put life in maturational perspective, to nurture the ongoing development of the mind, and ultimately to achieve psychological maturity. Without such models, we run the risk of becoming forever lost in the swamp of self-absorption, disorientation, stagnation, and, eventually, maturational arrest.

AVOIDING PREMATURE PERMANENT COMMITMENTS

By design, psychological maturation is preemptive in immaturity, making development a full-time job. Our society has always intuitively understood this; it has set aside time in the immature phase almost wholly for growing up. It is during this period that our children, adolescents, and young adults are educated, socialized, and provided with various "growing" experiences.

The needs associated with permanent commitments frequently conflict with the requirements of growing up. For this reason, consensual reality holds that permanent commitments to work, to relationships, to child rearing, and to life in general are best deferred until the end of immaturity. But when, exactly, is that? According to maturational theory, under optimal conditions, the immature phase actually extends into one's early thirties—lengthening by a full decade our current concept of the span of immaturity.

This is not a comfortable concept. Commitments to marriage, child rearing, and job or career are usually well under way by then. Indeed, our society is not structured to nurture and facilitate ongoing unencumbered maturation into mid- and late youth. The requirements of permanent commitments made during immaturity almost always compete with the needs of a mind still actively under construction. Resolving the dilemma of competing needs in favor of a commitment burdens the maturational process and poses a risk to becoming mature.

One final word: Should we become derailed by maturational detours, it does not necessarily mean all is lost. As long as the mind is under construction, it will attempt to get back on track—to get restarted, as it were. But once the mind succumbs to maturational arrest, there is no restarting. This leaves only two options for the remainder of the life cycle. One is for the person to withdraw into a comfortable, stationary niche—well removed from a world that requires additional development. (And until humankind advances a bit further along the maturational path, this is what happens— at some point—to most of us.) The other option is actively to try to stop the world from changing. This ablates the need for development that can never occur.

~ 14 ~

Implications

*W*hen it comes to "understanding" a subject, most of us take the natural, even obvious approach. We base our understanding on the way the subject appears. Ptolemaic theory is a classic example. It must have been reasonable—and certainly obvious—to believe that the sun revolved around the earth when that conclusion fit perfectly with the appearance of the sun arcing overhead.

Heliocentric theory, an intuitively derived mathematical model, contradicted Ptolemaic ideas and diverged completely from conventional reality. And by all accounts it was for a very long time a hard sell. Indeed, its current acceptance is not based on any change in what we see—for the sun still arcs overhead—but because it has proven to be sound theory. Today it is only one part of a mathematically established worldview that has enabled scientists to determine correctly much of the design of our universe.

Among the psychological theories concerned with maturation, learning theory is most reminiscent of Ptolemaic theory. Certainly it appears that children grow up primarily by learning what they are taught and by remembering their experiences. Indeed, the Freudian concept of a dynamic unconscious was not well received in late-nineteenth-century Vienna. Nor is our acceptance of it today based on appearance, for children still appear to grow up through learning. Rather, we accept the idea of a dynamic unconscious because we intuitively sense that growing up is rooted in a deep-seated process, and that nurturing this process is critical to developmental success.

Like its predecessors, learning and developmental theory, maturational theory sets out to explain how we become psychologically mature. Unlike its predecessors, it starts from the position that the process of becoming mature is not disclosed to us through observation. Rather, to understand it we must combine some kind of extraordinary psychological technique with intuitive input to isolate the process and then determine its fundamental design.

Maturational theory, the product of this coupling, now stands as an alternative to both learning and developmental theory. It advances a dramatically different design of the human life cycle, in which the first three decades are spent primarily in developing the system the mind uses to understand the world. Only when this system is complete is a person positioned to understand the world correctly and to actualize fully his or her potential in the wider world.

The implications of maturational theory are manifold. The ones I have chosen to discuss here are tied to three major facets of maturational theory: the maturational process itself; a mature thought process; and (in Chapter 15) the fundamental nature of our species.

The Implications of the Maturational Process

Up to now, the end points of psychological development have been rather nebulous: the capacity to assume responsibility, the readiness to earn a living and to parent, the capacity to resolve psychological conflict, to achieve and maintain internal harmony, the actualization of potential, and so on. Understanding the maturational process changes our general understanding of psychological development. By linking the process to the development of the mind, maturational theory redefines the critical steps along the maturational path. The implication here is that we—as parents and educators, or simply as individuals trying to grow up—must redesign the way we think about psychological maturation. Facilitating the maturational process now means nurturing the development of the mind.

Another implication of the maturational process is that relationships with others must be viewed not only from a social or interpersonal perspective but from a maturational one as well. Personal affinities from friendships to intimate relationships; a student's relationships with professors, mentors, and classmates; even one's relationship with religion or with a complex therapeutic process—all must now be seen as primarily in the service of advancing the process of constructing the mind.

Still another implication of the maturational process is that the development of the mind does not stop with the end of adolescence. With proper nurturing, one's capacity to understand the world continues to evolve until the establishment of psychological maturity. This means that the behaviors of early, middle, and late youth (midlife) are symbolic, and cannot be taken at face value. That is, most behavior throughout immaturity—just as the oppositional behavior of the two-year-old—is designed primarily to move the mind toward psychological maturity.

The Implications of a Mature Thought Process

ADULTHOOD AND LANGUAGE

There is a common perception nowadays that government does not work; that our laws do not deter crime; that our judicial system uses ineffective ways to arrive at truth; and that, at a practical level, our knowledge of psychology does not seem particularly helpful. How is it that as bright as we are as individuals, and as advanced and sophisticated as we are as a nation, we are still unable to find solutions to so many problems in areas of paramount importance to us? According to maturational theory, part of the reason is that the immature mind is not designed to think about these subjects correctly.

But the encouraging news is that the emergence of the stage of adulthood into the general population will provide us with a new resource: the capacity to understand our world in different ways. Adults—capable of processing input from all six senses—will be able to create an understanding of their world through a new psychological system that will enable them naturally to understand the inherent design of a subject. Understanding that design is the key that permits the mind to think about problems correctly—in ways that create solutions that work.

PROCESSING FROM THE WHOLE TO THE PART

In maturity we are able to understand a subject by first constructing the whole. The mind will then fill in the parts. At a tangible level, this reversal of the processing technique of immaturity means a different understanding of many subjects.

Let's take as an example the issue of abortion. Currently

the abortion debate revolves around the question of when a developing fetus becomes alive, becomes a human being. Is it when it has, say, a heartbeat? A human appearance? Movement in its limbs? Is it viability that marks the beginning of life? And if so, do we mean the natural viability that occurs during the third trimester of pregnancy, or the much earlier viability that can now be achieved through advanced medical technology?

The immature mind can start with any such point (the part) to make a case for the beginning of life. With a choice of arbitrary starting points, not only do natural differences of opinion exist but there is no way to resolve the issue through consensus.

By contrast, I submit that the mature mind will automatically create the understanding that life begins with the natural viability that occurs during the third trimester of pregnancy. That is when the fetus is "whole"—and this is the dynamic singularity the mature mind will use as a starting point in resolving the issue. Within this framework, other starting points will be viewed simply as wrong.

Thus, just as the knowledge "My thoughts come from me" or "I am responsible for my life" is inherent in the structure of the immature mind, the knowledge of when life begins conforms to a reality inherent in the structure of the mature mind. With this new understanding, there can, I believe, at last be a basis for consensus.

Indeed, at some future time, today's controversy over abortion will be looked upon as we now look upon the sixteenth-century controversy over the design of the universe. That controversy was resolved through the language of mathematics. I believe that today's controversy over the onset of life—along with many other pressing issues and seemingly unresolvable problems—can be brought to a natural conclusion only through the concepts created by the mature mind.

Part IV

~~~

~ 15 ~

Inherent Design and the Concept of Language

*I*n the spring of 1543, Nicholas Copernicus—mathematician, astronomer, Polish cleric—nearing the age of seventy, lay partially paralyzed from a series of strokes. It was only then, in the safe harbor of approaching death, that he could dare to publish his long-held belief in a sun-centered universe.

In doing so he broke with the false reality established by both everyday observation and religious fiat: that the sun, which was seen to rise, arc overhead, and then set, was circling the earth. By thus demoting the world and humankind from the centerpiece of God's creation, Copernicus was challenging the accepted wisdom and authority of the Roman Catholic Church—an authority preserved by the threat of being charged with heresy, and enforced when necessary through demands for recantation, torture, and death on the rack.

Reality in sixteenth-century southern Europe was based primarily on a mixture of personal experience, superstition, and divine knowledge conveyed through religious doctrine. By discarding the concept of an earth-centered universe, Copernicus opted for a model based on mathematical calculations. In the life of sixteenth-century humanity, this was a relatively new method of ascertaining truth. As a result, the sun-centered model of the solar system was understandably slow to win acceptance. Morris Kline, mathematician and historian, elaborates:

> At first only mathematicians supported the new theory. This is not surprising. Only a mathematician convinced that the universe was mathematically and simply designed would have had the mental fortitude to disregard the prevailing philosophical, religious, and scientific counter-arguments and to appreciate the mathematics of such a revolutionary astronomy. Only one possessed of unshakable convictions about the importance of mathematics in the design of the universe would have dared to affirm the new theory against the mass of powerful opposition it met.[1]

We now know, of course, that Copernicus was correct in choosing mathematics to construct the design of the solar system. But while correctly selecting a sun-centered model, he mistakenly committed to the religious belief that God, in his perfection, would create only perfectly circular orbits. This erroneous assumption shaped Copernicus's mathematics and produced a flawed theory of orbital design.

In 1609, over half a century later, a German-Lutheran mathematician, astrologer, and astronomer addressed the problem. Like Copernicus, Johannes Kepler took a mathematically based approach to problem solving, but he was not unduly burdened by the concept of heavenly perfection. Kepler determined that the planets follow elliptical orbits about the central sun. Our knowledge of the orbital configuration of the solar system was now correct; and, perhaps equally important, the correctness of mathematically based design in nature was established.

Today we accept without question the model of a sun-centered solar system, even though the sun still appears to circle overhead. We similarly accept the mathematically derived proposition that we stand on a rapidly spinning globe, although we feel no hint of its movement. And we know that gravity keeps us firmly planted on the earth's spinning surface, although we feel no indication of its pull.

Mathematically based designs replace the subjective, descriptive language of observation and religion with objective, measurable concepts: specific distances, angles, degrees of arc, for example. It is in these objective concepts, spelled out in the language of mathematics, that much of the design of our physical world is written. Moreover, the persuasiveness of this mathematical reality is rooted in two core characteristics: its demonstrated accuracy in conveying design and its capacity to provide a basis for verifying its correctness through prediction, independent testing, and proof.

Understanding basic design is for scientists, however, more than the elevated pursuit of correctness. We know that accurately understanding design through mathematics permits us to actualize the potential within a given area of inquiry. Thus the discoveries of Copernicus and Kepler, significant as they are, have served even more importantly as a starting point for greater knowledge: for understanding the seasons and the tides; for forecasting the weather; for formulating the specific relationships of planetary bodies, which enable us to explore space and to land on the moon.

Another historical example of the actualization of potential through the use of mathematics occurred in the late eighteenth and early nineteenth centuries. The original attempt to understand the composition of material was set forth in numerous theories known as alchemy. In 1787, Antoine Lavoisier suggested that all material is composed of elements, molecules, compounds, and mixtures. Relying on mathematically based concepts such as the conservation of matter, he accurately determined the fundamental design of material. In so doing, he provided the conceptual basis for transforming the prescience of alchemy into the science of chemistry. Correctly understanding the design of matter permitted early chemists to make a series of discoveries we refer to as the chemical revolution. Today, advances in chemistry from synthetic materials to designer pharmaceuticals reflect only a tiny fraction of the potential actualized in over two centuries of scientific development.

Indeed, the potential actualized in such fields as chemistry, physics, biology, and engineering—fields which have contributed most of the advances that distinguish our civilization from that of the ancient Greeks—can be directly or indirectly attributed to the use of mathematics. Yet no tool analogous to the language of mathematics has ever been discovered within the social or behavioral sciences. In such fields as psychology, sociology, political science, and law, simple descriptive language still determines our understanding of all fundamental design.

Equilibrium and Language

Let us for a moment examine how maturational theory enables us to address the concept of language by looking at its formation from the perspective of the developing mind. According to this theory, in each type of advanced equilibrium—dyadic and independent—the mind has its own method of creating language.

DYADIC EQUILIBRIUM AND IDEAS

In dyadic equilibrium, the mind processes information by using mostly perceptual input and by expanding the part to the whole. This means that understanding any subject has its origin in how some part of it looks, sounds, feels, tastes, or smells. The mind then transforms that understanding into language that can be spoken. Maturational theory calls this a *form-based language*, because the mind creates its understanding of the subject from what it experiences as a bit of form.

A form-based language conveys ideas—a descriptive impression of a subject rather than a complete and accurate understanding of it. The number of ideas about any subject is virtually infinite, because input from any of the five senses can combine with any starting point (bit of form) to create one's own personal idea. Moreover, ideas change as both the perception of a subject and the starting point change. Finally, although we generally experience ideas as being correct and sufficient, they do not provide a reliable basis for prediction. Therefore, *scientifically* verifying an idea is not possible.

But with regard to the developing mind, ideas were never intended to create an accurate understanding of a complex world. Rather, they are designed to provide an interim basis for understanding while the mind is still under construction. And frequently the limitations built into the structure of an idea can be helpful. For example, there is comfort in believing that any given idea is sufficient and correct, because this belief obscures the limited nature of any understanding. Having many ideas about a subject may also facilitate processing, a method of problem solving in which ideas from various starting points are distilled to yield one solution.

Moreover, in immaturity we want our ideas to evolve as we

develop along the maturational path. Indeed, a compelling argument can be made for the proposition that one would have to stay in a maturationally fixed position in order to remain faithful, over time, to any given idea.

With this preamble in place, I suggest that learning theory and developmental theory are both collections of ideas. Developmental theory is simply a better set of ideas than those of learning theory, because its tenets better conform to our observations of human behavior.

INDEPENDENT EQUILIBRIUM AND LANGUAGE

In independent equilibrium, as we know, the mature mind automatically uses intuitive input to process information. As a result, the world is experienced as a collection of dynamic singularities rather than an amalgam of ideas. This is simply the form that the dynamic world takes—just as the world experienced by the perceptual senses is one of size, shape, color, texture, sound, and so on. Each dynamic singularity becomes a starting point in the understanding of this dynamically based world. As such, the starting point is a whole. For example, all of psychological maturation is a dynamic singularity, and the entity can easily be conceptualized by any mature person who has moderate talent in the field of psychology. The aspect of psychological maturation that deals with the development of the maturational path is also a dynamic singularity. It is this singularity that has been the subject of this book.

And just as the mind in dyadic equilibrium transforms its perceptually based understanding of the world into a spoken, form-based language, so the mind in independent equilibrium transforms its intuitively based understanding into a spoken language. Maturational theory calls this a *dynamically based language*, because the mind experiences the origin of this understanding as fundamentally dynamic.

The Language of Science

We know that intuition plays an important role in understanding the world of the physical sciences. Einstein pointed to its importance in his often quoted explanation of why he chose physics over mathematics: "My intuition was not strong enough in the field of mathematics to differentiate clearly the fundamentally important, that which is really basic, from the rest of the more or less dispensable erudition."[2] Mathematician Morris Kline expresses his belief: "Certainly, mathematical creation is furthered most by men who are distinguished by their power of intuition rather than by their capacity to make rigorous proofs."[3]

Also acknowledged, but less well documented, is the relationship between understanding and the processing style of beginning with the whole and filling in the parts. One of the most interesting accounts of this style was provided in the 1860s by the Scots physicist James Clerk Maxwell. Maxwell committed Michael Faraday's vision of lines of force to mathematics and thus defined the relationship between electricity and magnetism. Maxwell's theory then initiated its own scientific revolution—an event comparable to the chemical revolution. Maxwell wrote of Faraday's thought process and the issue of "starting from the whole":

For instance, Faraday, in his mind's eye, saw lines of force traversing all space where the mathematicians saw centres of force attracting at a distance: Faraday saw a medium where they saw nothing but distance: Faraday sought the seat of the phenomena in real actions going on in the medium, they were satisfied that they had found it in a power of action at a distance impressed on the electric fluids.

When I had translated what I considered to be Faraday's ideas into a mathematical form, I found that in general the results of the two methods coincided . . . but that Faraday's methods resembled those in which we begin with the whole and arrive at the parts by analysis, while the ordinary mathematical methods were founded on the principle of beginning with the parts and building up the whole by synthesis.[4]

A Sequence of Discovery

I have chosen these illustrations to bring into focus four elements frequently associated with the process of discovery: the importance of intuition; the use of the whole as a beginning point; the role of mathematics as a language; and the actualization of potential.

I suggest that scientific discoveries often result from the use of intuitive input combined with the cognitive style of beginning with the whole (frequently expressed as a revelation) and filling in the parts. This style of processing isolates dynamic singularities. Once a dynamic singularity is isolated, the mind determines its inherent design and transforms it into dynamically based language. If this particular dynamic singularity falls within the purview of the physical sciences, the information will be encoded in mathematical symbols— making mathematics the language scientists must use. Discerning the inherent design of a subject becomes the critical first step in the process of fully actualizing potential. (See Figure 15.)

Intuitive input + beginning with the whole →

  dynamic singularities →

    inherent design →

      dynamically based language →

        scientific discovery →

          actualization of potential[5]

A Sequence of Scientific Discovery
FIGURE 15

The Mature Mind and Language

I have interjected these few sections because the mature mind routinely uses the same processing sequence in everyday life: It isolates dynamic singularities, determines their inherent design, and transforms this information into a dynamically based language. But for most of us, the world being processed is the everyday world of work, relationships, social and political issues, personal development, and so on. Unlike the physical world, which is encoded in mathematical symbols, the design of this world is encoded in the symbols of a spoken language.

This means that there are two different categories of spoken languages: One is the form-based language of immaturity, the language created by the incomplete mind under construction, a language of ideas. The other is the dynamically based language of maturity, the language created by the fully formed mind. According to maturational theory, this is the language that naturally conveys the inherent design of those aspects of our world expressed by a spoken language. I

187

further suggest that here, as in the physical world, understanding inherent design is the critical first step in fully actualizing potential. If this is true, then the spoken language of maturity is to life in the everyday world as mathematics is to the physical world. Both convey inherent design and, in turn, act as the first step in the actualization of potential.

Finally, dynamically based language is not merely an elaboration of the form-based language of immaturity. Rather, it is different in kind. It conveys a world that the immature mind does not normally see. It is created by a psychological process that the immature mind does not possess. And it will enable our species to accomplish something that ideas alone never can: the actualization of potential in the world that is set forth in the spoken word.

Maturational Theory as an Example

I submit maturational theory as an example of a theory written in a dynamically based language that conveys the inherent design of the process of becoming psychologically mature through the spoken word. The theory covers many subjects that are themselves examples of dynamic singularities: the maturational path; immaturity and maturity; childhood, adolescence, youth, and adulthood; the maturational process and the concept of language, to name but a few. Furthermore, the inherent design of these singularities is conveyed in such concepts as organizers, borrowing, type-1 abilities, and the sequential unfolding of steps.

I further submit that the capacity to actualize individual potential fully depends upon correctly constructing the human mind. This task requires that each person successfully complete the steps in his or her maturational process, all the way from childhood to maturity. Accomplishing this sequence requires a comprehensive and correct understanding of the maturational path and of the process responsible for movement along this path.

I believe that maturational theory supplies such an understanding—that it is that map.

Language, Prediction, and Proof

The concept of language offers an opportunity for proof not previously available in the behavioral sciences. Historically, end points such as happiness or the capacity to love and work have proven too "soft" to act as valid criteria for prediction and proof. We are happy one day, unhappy the next; we work hard one day but are unable to work well the next. Even if the maturational path ended, say, in the ability to be socially responsible, on the issue of proof we would be no better off.

However, maturational theory states that with the accomplishment of maturity the mind becomes capable of creating concepts that are different in kind, and that these concepts enable us to actualize potential that could not otherwise be actualized in the world. This coupling creates a basis for prediction that does not exist in learning or developmental theory. A mature person either can or cannot create concepts different from those created in immaturity; and these concepts either do or do not enable one to actualize potential in the world. If both are realities, then, to my way of thinking, we have achieved a level of proof.

Implications

One final set of observations. If there is a preexisting path that comes to an end point with the capacity to create a language; and if this language, in turn, enables us (collectively) to understand the inherent design of our world and actualize the potential within it, then this sequence is a plan.[6] And if so this raises other questions for which humankind has long sought answers—answers beyond the scope of this book:

Does a plan imply a planner?

Does a plan suggest that our species has a predetermined, central role in the evolution of our planet?

Is the development of the human mind evidence of the hand of God?

Appendix

Life Phase	Immaturity			Maturity
Stage of Life	Childhood	Adolescence	Youth	Adulthood
Normative Crisis	Oedipal	Identity	Midlife	
Defining Cognitive Characteristic	Concrete Thinking	Abstract Thinking	Relativistic Thinking — Simple / Contextual	Nonlinear Thinking
Type of Understanding	Interim			Fully correct
Characteristic Language	Form-based			Dynamically based
Primary Orientation	Constructing a Mature Mind			Constructing One's Life in the World — Search for Individuality
Symbolic Behaviors	Oppositionality, Voyeurism, Exhibitionism, Play, Work, Independent Action	Coupling & Uncoupling, Rebelliousness	Marriage & Divorce, Sex, Running & Fitness, Work, Isolation, Alienation	
Sample Type-1 Abilities	Good	Self as Singular	Dynamic Singularity, Self as Whole	
Capacity to Conceptualize	No			
Age	0 5 10	15	20 25	30

Human Life Cycle

(From Birth Through the Accomplishment of Psychological Maturity)

Glossary

Abstract thinking: Hypothetical and deductive reasoning, the emergence of which signals the onset of adolescence as a stage of life.

Actualization: The fourth step in a five-step sequence through which the mind develops new psychological abilities. It is the act of giving form to a newly emerging ability, and it determines whether the ability will be correctly formed or compromised.

Actualize potential: To develop progressively the innate potential within a subject.

Actualizer: A person who assists in the development of a newly emerging type-1 ability by first appearing to understand the ability and then providing the permission to complete its development.

Adolescence: The stage of life following childhood, which begins with the emergence of the capacity to think abstractly and ends with the successful resolution of the identity crisis. Neither event can be tied to a specific chronological age.

Adulthood: Following youth, it is the fourth stage of life and is characterized by the mind's capacity to think in nonlinear terms. Adulthood begins with the successful resolution of the midlife crisis and may extend throughout the remainder of the life span.

Alienation: Oppositional symbolic behavior exhibited in youth, which functions as a means of retiring the context carrier.

Basic competency: The end point in the construction of any one of the mind's six areas of basic functioning, or the fulfillment of any one of the mind's six basic needs. Once basic competency is achieved, type-1 abilities in that area are capable of correctly functioning in the mature mind, and additional type-1 ability development in that area is no longer required.

Borrowing: An action of the maturational process in which the mind fills an internal void by treating an external person or thing as if it were a part of the mind. Indications of borrowing may be dependency, possessiveness, and the need to have control over the person or thing being borrowed.

Carrier: See S_1 *carrier.*

Checking-in behavior: Reestablishing contact with an organizer in order to maintain an internal state of consolidation.

Childhood: The first stage of life in the human life cycle, characterized by concrete thinking.

Compartmentalization: A method of diminishing mental tension by treating a substantial range as if it were made up of separate sections or compartments.

Concrete thinking: Conceptualizing the world in literal terms.

Consensual reality: A belief system shared by a large number of people who correctly or incorrectly accept it as reality.

Consolidation: An action in which the mind unconsciously experiences psychological abilities as associating or gathering together. In immaturity, consolidation results in psychological stability.

Constancy: The capacity of an S_1 carrier to maintain psychological equilibrium without the presence of an organizer. There are five types of constancy, one for each type of S_1 carrier.

Contextual thinking: A form of relativistic thinking that develops in late youth. In it the mind is able to place a topic within a broadened area or field rather than view it from a simple or discrete position.

Conventional relationships: Relationships that, because they are not symbolic, can be taken at face value.

Developmental arrest: See *Maturational arrest.*

Developmental crisis: A normal and usually protracted period of psychological instability. Three such periods occur during immaturity: the Oedipal crisis, the identity crisis, and the midlife crisis.

Developmental process: A gradually unfolding, unconscious process that, according to developmental theory, creates the psychological abilities needed to become psychologically mature. It is in many ways analogous to the maturational process of maturational theory.

Developmental theory: A theory which holds that psychological maturation occurs as a consequence of an unconscious, unfolding process. This theory describes an inside-out process: that is, the abilities responsible for psychological growth originate within the mind.

Dyadic equilibrium: A type of equilibrium in which the mind remains consolidated through the use of organizers in the outside world. Dyadic equilibrium develops during the first three to five years of life and remains the characteristic way of achieving psychological stability throughout immaturity.

Dynamic dimension: That nonstatic dimension of a subject which is intuitively grasped and is somehow involved in or related to the subject's process of progressive change.

Dynamic singularity: The basic appearance in the mind's eye of the whole of a subject—formed only through the use of input from all six senses.

Dynamically based: A conceptualization derived primarily through intuition. (Its usage usually applies to language or theory.)

Equilibrium: An interrelationship or configuration among type-1 abilities that in more advanced forms results in psychological stability.

Form-based: A conceptualization derived primarily through perception. (Its usage usually applies to language or theory.)

Formula: See *Maturational formula.*

Free association: The psychoanalytic technique introduced by Sigmund Freud in which a patient says to the analyst whatever comes to mind. Its primary usage is to treat psychological problems stemming from compromised development that occurred during the first few years of life.

Fully correct understanding: The type of understanding created by the mature mind. It is characterized by the capacity to experience and process input from all six senses.

Fundamental design: The inherent structure and principles of functioning within a dynamic singularity.

Group A: Contains the abilities that fulfill the first three of six psychological needs crucial to creating the mind's fundamental understanding of a subject. They are to create stability, to experience all input, and to process information.

Group B: Contains the abilities that fulfill the fourth of six psychological needs crucial to creating the mind's fundamental understanding of a subject: the need to develop new type-1 abilities.

Group C: Contains the abilities that fulfill the final two psychological needs crucial to creating the mind's fundamental understanding of a subject. They are to create concepts and to form relationships.

Identity crisis: The second period of normal crisis in immaturity, specifically, the turbulent and unstable period of late adolescence in which the maturing person struggles to form and solidify a sense of identity. Once formed, this sense of identity— along with the sense that "I can borrow from myself"—ends the crisis. The development of a sense of identity is an indicator of the transformation from adolescence into youth.

Independent equilibrium: A type of psychological equilibrium in which stability is maintained without the use of outside people or things as organizers. Independent equilibrium is brought about through the use of the S_2 carrier and characterizes psychological maturity.

Inherent design: See *Fundamental design.*

Instability: See *Psychological instability.*

Interim understanding: An incomplete understanding of the world created by the mind of immaturity. It is constructed through input from the first five (perceptual) senses and is characterized by processing information from the part to the whole.

Intuition: The mind's sixth sense. Intuitive input enables the mind to experience change fully. This change is sometimes referred to as the dynamic dimension of a subject.

Learning theory: The theory that the mind matures primarily through its capacity to remember. It is an "outside-in" theory; that is, it holds that information that evokes psychological change comes from the "outside."

Life cycle model: A theoretical model that depicts psychological maturation from birth to death. The stage-of-life model is one example.

Maturational arrest: The phenomenon in which the progressive development of type-1 abilities ceases, thereby stunting subsequent psychological maturation.

Maturational formula: The method through which the mind expands its understanding of the world. Using a repetitive pattern, the mind extends the portion of the world it experiences as psychologically real and then develops the abilities it needs to deal with the new range.

Maturationally based free association: A therapeutic technique in which a person says whatever comes to mind until the mind forms a type-1 ability.

Maturational path: The emerging sequence of type-1 abilities that culminates in the construction of the mature mind.

Maturational process: The component of the mind responsible for progressively constructing its capacity to create a fully correct understanding of a subject. It does this by (1) expanding the mind's range of understanding; (2) establishing enough type-1 abilities ultimately to produce a mature mind; (3) facilitating movement along the maturational path through tension reduction; and (4) promoting adherence to the path.

Maturational theory: A theory of psychological development which holds that the central achievement of immaturity is the construction of the mind's capacity to create a fully correct understanding of the world.

Maturity: See *Psychological maturity.*

Midlife crisis: The third and last period of normal crisis in immaturity, specifically, the period of turbulence and instability in late youth that occurs as the mind develops the capacity to process intuitive input. Its resolution establishes the person in adulthood and maturity.

Negation: An action of the maturational process through which the mind diminishes the tension resulting from a disparity between range and type-1 abilities available to deal with that range. In negation the mind treats an established part of itself as if it does not exist.

Neurosis: The failure of the mind to outgrow the need for the maternal and paternal carriers in order to maintain dyadic equilibrium.

Oedipal crisis: The first of three normal crisis periods in immaturity. It occurs at about age five, as the mind is stabilizing its capacity to create an interim understanding of the world.

Optimal tension: The tension level at which the maturational process best functions.

Organizer: An external person or thing, activity or idea that stimulates the S_1 carrier to consolidate type-1 abilities into a state of dyadic equilibrium.

Point of abandonment: A time during the immature phase of the life cycle when one chooses to abandon the maturational path in favor of prematurely pursuing one's life in the world. This choice attenuates the maturational process and results in maturational arrest.

Practicing behavior: Repetitive activity that displays a newly emerging type-1 ability. It is the means through which the mind understands how an emerging ability functions. Practicing behavior is the third step of the five-step sequence through which psychological abilities are formed.

Principle of sufficiency: Holds that perfectly acceptable standards exist well short of the extreme, thereby freeing one from the need to have the most, the newest, the biggest, and so on.

Pseudoactualizer: A person chosen as an actualizer who subverts the development of a type-1 ability instead of facilitating it. His or her responses typically lead to compromised ability formation.

Psychoanalysis: A form of therapy that uses the technique of free association to help correct psychological problems originating primarily in the first few years of life.

Psychological ability: The most fundamental building block in the development of the mind, a skill or an action that enables the mind to perform differently—in a more advanced way—than before.

Psychological development: See *Psychological maturation.*

Psychological equilibrium: See *Equilibrium.*

Psychological growth: See *Psychological maturation.*

Psychological immaturity: The phase of the life cycle during which the mind progressively constructs its system for ultimately creating a fully correct understanding of the world. Until this system is complete, the mind utilizes input primarily from the first five senses to create an interim understanding of the world.

Immaturity, which can be divided into three stages—childhood, adolescence, and youth—is further characterized by (1) the ongoing development of type-1 abilities; (2) symbolic engagement in the world; (3) creation of an understanding of a subject by expanding the part to the whole; and (4) the preemptive need to pursue the maturational path.

Psychological instability: The inability to function well psychologically. It results from a loss of stable equilibrium.

Psychological maturation: The process through which the mind reaches the most complete state of development possible.

Psychological maturity: The phase of life that begins when the mind is positioned to create a fully correct understanding of the world. It is synonymous with adulthood and is characterized by, among other things: (1) the mind's use of input from all six senses; (2) nonlinear thinking; (3) creating an understanding of a subject by beginning with the whole and filling in the parts; (4) independent equilibrium; (5) the mind's development through type-2 ability formation; (6) the ability to take the world at face value, free from symbolic meaning; and (7) the preemptive need to actualize one's potential instead of following the maturational path.

Psychological skill: See *Psychological ability.*

Psychological stability: The ability to maintain a consistent state of equilibrium.

Psychoneurosis: See *Neurosis.*

Psychotherapy: Any formal attempt among two or more people to change psychological functioning.

Random walk: The pattern created by free movement among the various components of the maturational process.

Range: That portion of the world the mind can experience as real at any given time.

Rebellion: A form of adolescent behavior designed to purge the mind of its continuing use of mother and father carriers. It is characterized by acts intended to anger and disappoint the parents.

Relativistic thinking: The ability to conceptualize issues from diverse perspectives, various points of view, or different frames of reference. Its emergence signals the onset of youth.

Reworking: The process of resubmitting a type-1 ability to the five-step sequence through which it was developed. This is done in an effort to complete what was compromised in the original formation. Generally, the more recently formed and isolated the compromised ability, the easier it is to rework.

S_1 carrier: A special type-1 ability that functions as a magnet to draw and hold other psychological abilities together in order to effect consolidation. Its presence dictates that the mind will: (1) experience the world through the use of the five perceptual senses; (2) effect stability through the use of external organizers; and (3) create an understanding of a subject by expanding the part to the whole.

S_2 carrier: A special type-1 ability that functions to align input from all six senses with the mind's capacity to process information. It is the functional centerpiece of the psychologically mature mind's capacity to create a fully correct understanding of the world.

Self-actualizing: The act of developing a psychological ability within one's own mind—first through understanding a newly emerging ability and then through granting to oneself permission to develop the ability. Achieving the capacity to self-actualize enables one to become self-developing and obviates the need for outside actualizers.

Self-developing: The act of creating psychological abilities solely through one's own mind.

Stability: See *Psychological stability*.

Stage of life: Any of four stages of the life cycle: childhood, adolescence, youth, and adulthood.

Stage of life model: Any model that subdivides the life cycle according to the stages of life.

Suspended equilibrium: The initial form of the mind, in which psychological abilities are too loosely associated to permit psychological stability.

Symbolic behavior: The kind of practicing behavior through which type-1 abilities are developed. The real purpose of the behavior is not apparent to the one engaging in the behavior or to others but must be decoded for the underlying meaning to be understood.

Symbolic engagement: The expressions of the maturational process that characterize type-1 ability development and that, although available to simple observation, must be decoded for the underlying meaning to be understood. Symbolic engagement has two components: symbolic behavior and symbolic reality.

Symbolic reality: The consciously experienced component of symbolic engagement.

Symbolic relationships: Relationships formed at least in part for the unconscious purpose of promoting psychological maturation. These relationships can be with other people, with oneself, one's job, places, belief systems, or any other ideas or "things."

Type-1 ability: A psychological ability that constructs the system the mind uses to understand the world. It is created through a five-step sequence in which symbolic engagement plays an integral role.

Type-2 ability: A psychological ability that enhances the understanding of the world the mind creates through type-1 ability formation. But, in contrast to the type-1 ability, its practicing phase is not concealed and therefore needs no decoding to be understood. As a consequence, type-2 development can be taken at face value.

Unconscious functioning: Psychological activity that occurs outside of awareness.

Youth: The stage of life that follows adolescence and is characterized by the ability to think relativistically. Youth continues throughout the third and into the fourth decade of life and ends with the successful resolution of the midlife crisis.

Zone of abandonment: The socially prescribed time during psychological immaturity when one is expected to assume adult responsibilities—embark on a career, marry, and/or have children. These actions, prematurely undertaken, can result in maturational arrest.

Notes

The epigraph by Albert Einstein is quoted in Werner Heisenberg, *Physics and Beyond: Encounters and Conversations* (New York: Harper and Row, 1971), p. 77.

Chapter 2

1. Today these disorders would be called psychoneuroses or, more commonly, neuroses.
2. Indeed, these two groups of abilities form the basis for the two leading branches of psychology: cognitive and object-relations.
3. This profile is remarkably similar to what existed in eighteenth-century alchemy, the prescientific phase of today's chemistry. Here, historians have noted there were about as many theories as there were practicing alchemists.
4. Anna Freud, Humberto Nagera, and W. Ernest Freud write about adults and adult developmental profiles: "In this instance assessment is concerned not with an ongoing process but with a finished product in which, by implication, the ultimate developmental stages should have been reached." "Metapsychological Assessments of the Adult Personality," *Psychoanalytic Study of the Child* 29, no. 9 (1965).
5. In their book *On Adult Development,* psychoanalytic theoreticians

Calvin A. Calurusso and Robert A. Nemiroff state as their third hypothesis: "Whereas childhood development is focused primarily on the formation of psychic structure, adult development is concerned with the continuing evolution of existing psychic structure and with its use" (New York: Plenum Press, 1981), p. 65.

6. Alan Lightman, "First Birth," in *Mysteries of Life and the Universe,* ed. by William H. Shore (New York: Harcourt Brace Jovanovich, 1992), p. 16.

Chapter 3

1. Type-1 and type-2 abilities will be explained and described throughout the book—most comprehensively in Chapter 6.

2. Behavioral scientists have known for a century that redeveloping compromised abilities is crucial to successful psychotherapy. Compromised abilities function as damaged parts. Everyone has some, and normally they go unnoticed. But in certain combinations they result in psychological conflict, symptoms, and/or dysfunction. Most psychotherapies "work" by redeveloping the underlying compromised abilities, thereby resolving the problem.

It is less well known that theoretical work uses a similar tack. By "viewing" an ability as it develops, or a compromised ability as it redevelops, the theoretician observes development in progress. Not surprisingly, it is the redeveloping component that most frequently permits one to view maturation that should occur early in life. And it is the knowledge gleaned from viewing this component that enables one to reconstruct the actions of the maturational process over the first two or more decades of life.

Maturationally based free association is unique in that it isolates and exposes only type-1 development and redevelopment. So its value rests on the premise that the type-1 ability is all that counts when creating a general understanding of psychological maturation.

3. Before this, after 4,000 to 5,000 hours of free association, I was able to isolate enough type-1 abilities to determine that they serve as fundamental building blocks in the construction of our psychological capacity to function "as a person"—to work, play, form relationships, and so on.

Over approximately 35,000 to 40,000 hours of free association, I was able to make a further observation: In addition to forming a psychological basis for our development "as a person," type-1 abilities collectively construct the means through which the mind creates a fundamental understanding of the world. This seemingly subtle distinction goes to the heart of the difference between developmental and maturational theory. Whereas developmental theory asks how any given ability bears upon one's development as a person, maturational theory asks how any given ability bears upon the development of the mind's capacity to understand the world.

Chapter 4

1. Erik Erikson, "Identity and the Life Cycle," *Psychological Issues,* vol. 1 (New York: International Universities Press, 1959).
2. Kenneth Keniston, "Youth: A 'New' Stage of Life," *The American Scholar* 39, no. 4 (Autumn 1970): 635.
3. Clarified in a personal conversation with the author in 1971.
4. In Keniston's theory, adulthood is used as a "plug" to fill in the period between youth, the last discovered "true" stage of life, and the end of the life span.
5. See note 2, above.
6. This model was originally created from a much expanded pool of observations derived through the use of maturationally based free association—a pool that included such information as known type-1 abilities; the order in which the abilities naturally develop; the practicing behaviors associated with each developing ability; and the contribution of each ability to the construction and functioning of the mind. This pool of observations served as a reservoir of all information pertaining to psychologi-

cal maturation. Tracking the construction of the capacity to understand produced a model consistently intrapsychic in origin. That is, the path to psychological maturity remains grounded in the sequential development of unconscious type-1 abilities and in their role in constructing the mind's capacity to understand, rather than in the ability to function in a socially responsible manner. This provided the opportunity to create an intrapsychic definition of psychological maturity.

7. Technically, maturational theory gives adulthood the status of a true stage of life.

Chapter 5

1. A predictable developmental sequence (frequently characterized as an unfolding process) creates uniformity in the way we conceptualize psychological maturation. This means that when we talk about becoming mature, we can all "read from the same page."

Chapter 6

1. Actually, the mind has six maturational needs. They will all be presented in Chapter 8.

2. The experience of consolidation does not mean that abilities within the mind physically move closer together, only that the unconscious experience is of their moving closer together.

3. Margaret Mahler, *On Human Symbiosis and the Vicissitudes of Individuation* (New York: International Universities Press, 1968).

4. The term *transitional object* was coined by Donald Winnicott in "Transitional Objects and Transitional Phenomena," *International Journal of Psycho-Analysis* 34 (1953): 89–97.

5. Some developmentalists place hearing and seeing in a different order. D. A. Freedman, C. Cannady, and J. S. Robinson, "Speech and Psychic Structure: A Reconsideration of Their Relation," *Journal of the American Psychoanalytic Association* 19 (1971): 765–79.

6. Unions between feelers and see-ers are common and, as one might guess, problem ridden. The dilemma of such a union is

that each person's mind relies on different input to understand the world, resulting in a different reading of the same situation. When there is a problem in the relationship, not only are a feeler and a see-er unable to find a solution to it, they can't even agree on its basic nature and cause. Consequently, each is left with the sense that he (or she) can't get through to the other.

This kind of conflict is typified by the comments of David and Kathy. Married for twenty-five years, they sought therapy when their last child left home for college. Kathy was particularly unhappy about the unwanted "distance" between the couple and about the fact that she felt their partnership had become, over the years, emotionally sterile—a "marriage of convenience." When she talked with David about her feelings, he couldn't see the problem.

"It's as though David isn't interested in me anymore," Kathy said. "I don't feel loved. In fact, I can't remember the last time he told me he loved me. If he'd only be more expressive about his feelings, I would feel loved."

"Why should I tell her what she should already know?" David asked. "She ought to know by now I love her. We've been married for twenty-five years. Anyone who stays married to a woman that long must love her! I just don't see that we have a serious problem."

This couple obviously interpreted their relationship from different perspectives, different kinds of input: Kathy's interpretation was skewed toward feeling, David's, toward seeing. She did not feel loved because he didn't do the types of things that register with feelers: verbalize his love for her, show his feelings through gifts and flowers, and so on. He didn't even realize there was a serious problem because the visible signs of a successful marriage were there for him: twenty-five years of being together, mutual interests, no major glitches, and so on.

7. The specific mechanism through which the part is transformed into the whole is not difficult to see. First, one part is experienced as context; as such, it creates the basic premise to which all other parts conform. Let us use as an example prejudice. In this example, a person's color, religion, sex, sexual orientation,

or other such characteristics, forms the context. Next, this characteristic (as context) is experienced as "bad." The mind now fits all other characteristics of that person into this "bad" mold. One's understanding of that person is then influenced by the basic premise. This means that no matter what one thinks about such a person, the overall impression will be that he or she is bad.

8. We used to consider children such as Jeff behavioral problems; under learning theory, they needed to be "taught to pay attention."

9. The word *structure* does not imply a physical structure, nor does it refer to any of the familiar components of psychoanalytic structural theory. Instead, I use it to mean a stable, functional configuration of psychological abilities.

10. All five carriers do this by imposing a sense of their own carrier type on the thoughts they carry. For example, a young boy's thoughts about his father, carried on the father carrier, enable him appropriately to experience his father as his father. Similarly, using a context carrier to think about toys in his room enables the boy to experience them as being in his environment.

As long as thoughts line up correctly with the carrier type—for example, if Mark is using his model carrier to think about his wife, Lisa (the concept of wife is a model), the system works well. The model carrier enables Mark automatically to experience Lisa as his wife. But sometimes thoughts do not match up correctly with the carrier being used. If Mark uses his mother carrier to think about Lisa, he will unconsciously misconceptualize Lisa and symbolically treat her as his mother. Not surprisingly, this configuration frequently reflects the presence of a neurosis.

Chapter 7

1. The first step—creating an ability in pure form—is part of the maturational process. The second—determining how to use this ability—is part of the general process of socialization, which is never fully completed.

2. Abraham Maslow coined the term *self-actualization*. However, his

usage refers to a more general process of actualizing all potential. Here the term refers to a specific step in the development
of psychological abilities.
3. People often borrow heavily from their organizers.
4. This can be viewed as a fifth function of the maturational process.
5. This walk, however, is random within a very limited context, for
the sequence of steps to be mastered is preset in that the available options must conform to the requirements of the maturational process. Stray too far beyond these options and the entire
process lapses into chaos, which ultimately sinks into the psychological darkness of maturational arrest.

Chapter 9

1. Although there must be an analogous example in the female
child, it is not yet clear to me.
2. Whereas oppositionality occurs with the early development of
the maternal carrier in early childhood, alienation occurs with
the early development of the context carrier in early youth. The
alienated youth is attempting to differentiate psychologically
between him- or herself and his or her context.

Chapter 10

1. This conclusion seems similar to Noam Chomsky's belief in a
"language organ."
2. Kenneth Keniston, "Youth: A 'New' Stage of Life," *The American
Scholar* 39, no. 4 (Autumn 1970): 632.
3. Ibid., p. 635.
4. Julian Jaynes, *The Origin of Consciousness in the Breakdown of the
Bicameral Mind* (Boston: Houghton Mifflin, 1976).

Chapter 12

1. James Gleick, *Chaos* (New York: Viking, 1988), pp. 23–24.
2. The term *realization of God* refers to a subjective sense that actualizing potential progressively discovers or effects God—much

in the way a person is realized through the actualization of his or her potential.

Chapter 15

1. Morris Kline, *Mathematics: The Loss of Certainty* (Oxford: Oxford University Press, 1980), pp. 40–41.

2. Albert Einstein, *Autobiographical Notes,* bilingual edition, ed. and trans. by Paul Arthur Schilpp (La Salle and Chicago: Open Court, 1979); originally vol. 7 of the Library of Living Philosophers, Evanston, Ill.

3. Kline, *Mathematics: The Loss of Certainty* (Oxford: Oxford University Press, 1980), p. 314.

4. James Clerk Maxwell, *Treatise* (1891. Rpt. New York: Dover, 1954), pp. ix–x.

5. Notice that in this sequence, the concept of inherent design is tied to the actualization of potential rather than to the more usual questions of whether inherent design actually exists in the world or is a figment of the human thought process. Although these issues may be important, the more practical question is whether understanding a specific design enables one to actualize its potential fully. Using this perspective, Lavoisier's discovery of elements, molecules, compounds, and mixtures certainly qualifies as the inherent design of material, because it precipitated the chemical revolution. And Maxwell's theory based on Faraday's discovery more than qualifies as a statement of inherent design, because it initiated a similar scientific revolution in electromagnetism.

6. Understanding that this is a plan is dependent on having developed the concept of a language. In the absence of this concept, the sequence appears to be adaptive.

Index

Abortion, 174–75
Abstract thinking, 24, 34–35, 38,
 42, 124, 125
Actualization, 81–82
 of potential, 186–87, 188, 189
 self-, 84, 146
Actualizers, 79, 81–83, 114, 145
 pseudoactualizers, 83
 seeking, 81
Adolescence:
 abstract thinking and, 34–35
 in development theory,
  34–35
  psychological maturation
  ending in, 16–17, 20
 expansion of range of the mind
  in, 105
 historically, 121–22, 124–26
 identity crisis in, 33–34
 independence, 24
 maturational theory's beliefs
  about development beyond,
  20, 154–55
 relationships in, 15
 stage of life labeled, discovery
  of, 121–22, 125–26

Adolescence: Its Psychology and Its
 Relation to Physiology,
 Anthropology, Sociology, Sex,
 Crime, Religion, and Education
 (Hall), 121–22
Adulthood, 43
 nonlinear thinking and, 154–55
 understanding of the world in,
  174
Alchemy, 181, 182
Alienation, 17, 123, 126
Alternatives, offering, 13
Articulation of words, loss of
 ability for, 141, 143
Attention deficit disorder, 67
Autonomy, sense of, 12, 13
Avoidance, 90, 93

Basic competency, achievement
 of, 142
Bicameral mind, 130–31, 132, 133
Body image:
 concept of, 110–11
 further development of, 127
Bonding, 10

211